PEUGEOT

205 **GTI**

PEUGEOT 205 GTI

THE ENTHUSIAST'S COMPANION

EDITOR: RAY HUTTON

MRP

MOTOR RACING PUBLICATIONS LTD
Unit 6, The Pilton Estate, 46 Pitlake, Croydon CR0 3RY, England.

ISBN 0 947981 18 7
First published 1987

Photosetting by Zee Creative Ltd., London SW 16
Printed in Great Britain by Netherwood, Dalton & Co. Ltd.,
Bradley Mills, Huddersfield, West Yorkshire

CONTENTS

For GTI enthusiasts only

Rarely has one model changed the image of a car manufacturer as much as the Peugeot 205GTI. Since its launch in 1984, more than 15,000 British owners have delighted in the bright performance and super-sharp handling of this smart hot hatchback.

This book is for those owners, and others who would like to join their growing ranks. It describes the origins and development of the 205GTI and the equivalent CTI Cabriolet. There is a technical analysis, an assessment of the first and latest versions by a highly-respected car tester, plus hints on how to keep the car in top form or modify it for even more performance and an individual look.

It isn't simply a history of the model, neither is it a dry workshop manual — though its investigation is thorough and it is full of information and advice on buying and running a 205GTI.

And, because its existence is linked directly to the GTI, there are two chapters on the short but glorious career of the Peugeot 205 Turbo 16 rally car. Quite intentionally, it has the looks of a GTI, but under the skin lurks a mid-mounted turbocharged engine and four-wheel drive. As rally watchers will know, it's quite a car!

We have brought together seven well-known specialist authors to present the 205GTI and Turbo 16 story. All have wide experience with these cars — three have run their own GTIs for an extended period. They are professional motoring writers but also, to a man, enthusiasts. So it is appropriate that they should contribute to this book specifically for Peugeot 205GTI fans: The Enthusiast's Companion.

GTI with a French accent

Ray Hutton tells how Peugeot set out to create a new image — and used their sparkling sports hatchback to lead the way

Sporting three-doors — plans for the 205 Turbo 16 rally car (above) previewed the style of the production 205GTI.

A question answers the 'why' of the 205GTI. If this had been a book about any previous Peugeot, would you have wanted to read it? Knowing that their image was at best conservative and that the marque had nothing to offer the car enthusiast, in the early 1980s, new Peugeot management embarked on a carefully planned strategy to change their place in the automotive world.

The key to that strategy was the 205. It would be a modern small hatchback of wide appeal, good to look at and rewarding to drive. Other manufacturers had shown that a sporting version was a way of increasing sales and enhancing the reputation of the range as a whole. Peugeot made their intentions very clear at the time of announcement in February 1983. Not only did they have a pretty new model to compete squarely with the Renault 5 that dominated the French sales charts, but they declared their intention to enter World Championship rallying with a similar-looking (but actually completely different) car. A sports road version was inevitable to complement this rallying activity.

The 205 Turbo 16 rally car was in fact the first clue to how a three-door 205 might look. When the production sports 205 came along we could see that the idea of making road and rally cars of the same flavour had worked beautifully. The important proportions were the same, a similar design of Speedline alloy

Inspiration for Peugeot's hot hatchback came from the Volkswagen Golf of the same name. By the time of launch it was clear that the 'Mark 2' Golf GTI would be larger than its predecessor, leaving a convenient gap in the market for the new Peugeot.

The main production lines for the 205GTI are in the Peugeot factory in Mulhouse, where highly automated machinery was installed for the 205 range. This is the robotized welding line for the floorpan.

wheel was adopted and the styling motifs were carried over.

Peugeot were not ashamed to follow the market lead of others. The red stripe theme that had started with the Volkswagen Golf GTI and been copied by virtually all the 'hot hatchbacks' was adopted wholeheartedly. Volkswagen were clearly on top in this newly emerging category, Peugeot had the same objective, so why not use the same GTI label? It was cheeky — but they already had a (rather mild) 205GT and the new model would have a fuel-injected engine.

Peugeot's product planners, headed by Marc Honore, identified the Golf GTI as achieving exactly what they sought. 'The ordinary Golf didn't sell very well in France, but the GTI did. It had *image*. And we knew that before ours came out, the Volkswagen would get bigger, so it left a place for us.'

The 205 is small compared with the Golf GTI, Escort XR3i and Astra GTE. In fact, it is an in-between size which causes it to be matched against this group

The GTI's immediate predecessors in the Peugeot model line up were the sporting versions of the 104, like this 104S. Engines and transmission units were carried over from the 104 for the lower-powered versions of the 205.

and also the high-performance superminis like the Fiat Uno Turbo, Ford Fiesta XR2 and MG Metro Turbo. Price-wise, as the Golf has gone up-market the Peugeot has taken its place as the fashionable street racer for the enthusiast on a budget. Peugeot are very conscious of that position, hence the introduction of the 1.9-litre version as an additional model rather than a replacement for the original 1.6.

Such precise model planning did not seem possible in the late 1970s after the Peugeot Group, PSA, had taken over what had been Chrysler Europe. The acquisition of Chrysler's facilities made Peugeot, including Citroën, which they had absorbed in 1974, Europe's biggest car producers at the time. Looking back, it seems like 'size for size sake' and not long after the enlarged group was formed, the car businesss took a down-turn and PSA were left with an uncomfortable amount of the excess production capacity that we hear so much about.

All Chrysler's models had Peugeot equivalents and at first it seemed that they would continue to offer them all and let the buying public decide which they preferred. The Chryslers were renamed Talbots, but it didn't make much difference; Peugeot design influence was only apparent at the bottom of the Talbot range, where a variant of the 104 was introduced as the Samba.

In the old days, the family firm of Peugeot were private, almost secret, in the way they went about their business. Their cars were admirable in many ways — comfortable and tough, qualities that made them first choice as taxis in France and well received in several parts of Africa. That led to sorties into the Safari Rally, which was emerging as a major motor sporting event. Peugeot 404s and 504s, driven by wily locals, did consistently well in the Safari. Peugeot recognized the value of these achievements and in the 1970s started to field a works team in events where endurance was more important than out-and-out speed. They hired some of the best international drivers and, using specially-prepared 504 Coupes with V6 engines, were able to score a Safari win as late as 1978.

Talbot, née Chrysler, had pursued a more prominent motor sport policy. As Simca they had been associated with the Matra Formula 1 and sports car racing teams in the early 1970s, and the association was revived when Matra engines were re-adopted by Ligier for Grand Prix racing in 1981. Furthermore, the UK arm of the company had pushed for, and produced, a Lotus-engined version of the rear-wheel-drive Sunbeam hatchback, which turned out to be a highly competitive international rally car in the last year or two before the Audi Quattro changed the shape of rallying.

By 1982, it was clear that the idea of running Peugeot and Talbot as two separate companies within the Group was not going to work. What the French like to call a 'federation' between the marques was formed, so that the two

Peugeot's associate marque within the PSA Group, Talbot, had sought a more overtly sporting image in the early 1980s with the Sunbeam-Lotus rally programme and sponsorship of the Ligier-Matra Formula 1 team.

Minor variations — outwardly, there is little to distinguish the original UK-market 205GTI, with 105bhp 1.6-litre engine (above), from the 1986 115bhp model (below). Indicator repeaters on the front wings are a visual clue to the later car, which had two door mirrors as standard.

ranges would be integrated (Citroën would be, and has remained, separate from a marketing point-of-view). Though they didn't say so at the time, it was clear that when existing models had run their course Talbot would disappear. The name Peugeot — a proud one that goes back to the dawn of motoring — would meet the market alone.

PSA had already made moves towards centralizing their product development by setting up a modern Technical Centre in an old factory at La Garenne, not far from Paris. A five-year plan was devised to encompass all the Group's car lines and provide four basic chassis platforms and four engine families as well as a wide range of major and minor components as 'building blocks'. Today, all new Peugeots and Citroëns start life at La Garenne, the same engineers working on the mechanical design irrespective of the marque involved and drawing on this common component source.

The original design for the 205, however, preceded this rationalization. As Project M24, it was to be the replacement for the Peugeot 104 and was the subject of a 'notice of orientation' (the document that describes the required size, market segment and so on) in 1978, before the Chrysler takeover was finalized. To begin with, the thought was that the 104 platform would be retained, but eventually it was decided that M24 would be all-new. One result of that was that the new, bigger base would allow some expansion for a larger version, though at that time such a car was not in prospect. Later, C28, the

Side badging tells that this is the 1.9-litre model, introduced for the 1987 model year. New and distinctive alloy wheels of larger diameter, wearing lower-profile tyres, are the main identification point for the new 130bhp model.

Advertising approaches — French TV commercial (above) was a James Bond spoof that did not amuse the makers of the helicopter that the 205GTI out-ran. Side-by-side Press advert with the roadgoing 205 Turbo 16 was a neat link with the rally programme that demonstrated the visual similarity of the two very different cars.

Talbot Horizon replacement, was to make use of M24's room to expand and become the Peugeot 309.

Three and five-door versions of M24 were anticipated from the start, but Peugeot had initially planned to concentrate on the five-door (the most popular configuration for small cars in France and Spain). 'At one time the GTI was to have been the only three-door 205,' remembers Marc Honore. 'Only later did we decide to use the three-door shell throughout the range.'

Like Honore, many of the Peugeot management in this new phase of the Group's development had come from Chrysler. They drove forward an aggressive new publicity campaign to tell the public that things were changing. The 205 Turbo 16 rally car, shown well before it was ready to compete, was part of that. Adverts proclaimed: 'A constructor shows its claws', referring to Peugeot's lion symbol, and declared 205 'Un sacre numero', which doesn't quite mean a 'sacred number', rather 'What a number!'. Either way, the point was made: Peugeot's on the move.

Having launched with five versions of the five-door 205, including a 1,360cc GT, they decided to introduce additions to the range at six-monthly intervals. I attended an informal preview of one of these, the excellent 205 Diesel, at the Peugeot factory concealed in the Forest of Harth near Mulhouse, in Alsace, very close to the Swiss border. That was in autumn 1983, and after examining the renewed production lines where 205 production was in full swing, I was

In a different way, Peugeot's sporting and youthful image was enhanced by the introduction of a Cabriolet model in 1986. Two engine options were offered in France, but only the CTI, with GTI power-train, was made with right-hand drive. The Cabriolet's development is covered in Chapter 4.

invited to take a spin in the countryside in what looked to be an ordinary 205GT. Without further explanation, I was told that I would be met for tea and talks at a cafe some 30 miles away.

Though I had already been impressed by the 205, this one went like no other I had tried. A glance under the bonnet showed the reason — a fuel-injected 1.6-litre engine, which like the diesel that was the reason for my visit, had its gearbox alongside rather than underneath the engine, as in lesser 205s. I was told it delivered about 100bhp.

Later that day, I was shown, in great secrecy, one of the early running prototypes of the GTI. I remember thinking that Peugeot had gone overboard for bright colours and 'sports' badging and that this showed a confident change from their sober old days. But I was left in little doubt that the 205GTI, when it went public six months later, would be a great success.

Incidentally, just as the three-door body was planned for the GTI alone, it was never intended that there should be a five-door GTI. In fact, the wheels won't

The Peugeot 205 was available in 23 varieties by the end of 1985, led by the GTI and the Turbo 16 (in two versions) in the foreground.

Sports of other sorts — the three-door 205 body quickly spread from GTI to cheaper models in the range. The special edition carrying the distinctive logo of the Lacoste sportswear firm and finished in white with green trim used the 1.4-litre GT engine, while the 205XS, introduced for the 1987 model year, included the GT engine and several GTI features.

fit. But a run of a dozen five-door 205GRs were equipped with GTI running gear (and ¹/₂in narrower, 13in diameter wheels) for 'Q-car' use by the *gendarmerie*.

When the 205GTI did come out in the open it was for the official Press preview in the hills of southern Spain. Switchback mountain roads were ideal to show off the car's nimbleness and kart-like handling and the new model received high praise from virtually everyone who attended — though with some criticism of the ride. *Autocar* called it 'the worst riding Peugeot in recent history', but went on to say that they were not really complaining; it was the cost of a 'quantum leap' in handling. It was also a surprise, for the idea of a taut, hard-riding sports car from Peugeot, of all people, was something new. *Autocar* concluded that the 205GTI had 'the strongest claim to date to be considered the legitimate successor to the late, lamented Mini-Cooper S'.

The 205 had quickly moved into third place in the French sales charts. By the end of its first year it was the country's best-seller. The GTI was expected to take perhaps 10% of 205 sales. In practice, it averaged 11% in France over its first two years. Nearly 40% of the 40,000+ made a year are exported. When it first went on sale in Britain in June 1984, demand exceeded supply. Tod Evans, Peugeot Talbot's UK sales boss, predicted that 15% of 205s sold here would be GTIs by early 1985. The proportion has since risen to nearly 20%.

Evans was delighted to have such a car to sell: 'The 205GTI moves us into a sector that is young, dynamic and potentially profitable', he said at the car's UK launch. 'It's an area where we can enthusiastically stake our claim. We are dealing with a group of customers who are very knowledgeable about cars. They are interested in technical facts and they know about performance comparisons. They are dynamic and ambitious — and they probably haven't previously considered buying a Peugeot...'

Fostering that dynamic image got Peugeot into trouble in France. They decided on a 'James Bond' theme for a television advertising campaign. The resulting commercial, never screened in Britain, was one of the most ambitious ever made. It was filmed in the Kalahari desert and shows a GTI scampering past exploding landmines, shrugging off a rocket-firing helicopter, narrowly missing a speeding train, and finally diving off a cliff to land safely by parachute, whereupon the driver tidies his bow tie and sets off for a normal day's posing.

All good fun — only Aerospatiale, the makers of the Gazelle helicopter used in the film, didn't think so. They complained that their machine emerged in a very poor light. It was a nonsense, said the planemakers, to show a car out-running their 185mph helicopter. Distress rockets had been used to simulate heat-seeking missiles; the real things wouldn't have missed...

One might have thought that after a grumble all of this would be forgotten, but Aerospatiale reckoned it was bad for their arms business and brought pressure to bear through the higher echelons of the French Government. Peugeot were obliged to withdraw the advertisement, which had cost millions of francs, damaged two helicopters and wrecked a fleet of 205GTIs.

The Press adverts showing the GTI alongside an undecorated Turbo 16 rally car caused no such controversy, but carried through the sporting theme perfectly. It wasn't long before the four-wheel-drive supercar had some results to boast about as well and, to the company's great delight, the news media invariably referred to it simply as a Peugeot 205. The rally-linked promotional

Peugeot 309, basically an enlarged 205, has two counterparts to the GTI — the five-door 309 Injection is a UK-market special, using the 115bhp 1.6-litre engine, and the three-door 309GTI, new in 1987, makes use of the 130bhp unit from the 1.9.

plan, a personal commitment of Automobiles Peugeot president Jean Boillot, worked like a dream.

With the GTI well established, Peugeot felt able to utilize the three-door bodyshell for other purposes. First it gave rise to a range of cheaper X-series 205 variants. A pretty white-and-green Lacoste special edition followed, and gradually a full complement of three-doors included a version of the GT, the XS, with the 80bhp 1,360cc engine and a number of features of the GTI. It forms a kind of halfway house to the real thing.

Competition in the market meant that the GTI's 105bhp seemed on the low side by the end of 1985, so early in 1986 the standard engine was uprated to 115bhp by some detail cylinder head modifications and altered valve timing. A year earlier a shock absorber specification change had been introduced in an attempt to sweeten the ride harshness just a little. It worked, and any very slight loss of handling response when driving hard was compensated by improved comfort in normal conditions.

The introduction of the 16-valve Golf GTI and the Ford Escort RS Turbo, as well as increasing competition in the smaller class from cars like the new

Renault 5 Turbo, suggested that an even more powerful version was needed to keep the 205GTI up at the head of the pack. Hence the 1.9, introduced in France in October 1986 as an additional model, offering 130bhp, disc brakes all round, and wider, larger-diameter wheels carrying chunkier tyres.

The success of the 205 has led Peugeot to adopt the same formula for other models. By fitting the same fuel-injected engine in the Citroën Visa (originally based on the Peugeot 104), that became a GTI. Even closer to home, the 205's bigger brother, the 309, gained the 1.6-litre engine for its five-door SR Injection model before the 1987 arrival of the three-door variants and a fully-fledged 1.9-litre 309GTI. These days there is even a GTI version of the elderly Peugeot 505 saloon.

'You know,' says Marc Honore, reflecting on how the sporting 205 came into being, 'in France, GTI means PSA now, not Golf.'

Direct relative from the other side of the PSA group is the Citroën Visa GTI, which started with the 105bhp engine and inherited the up-rated 115bhp 1.6-litre at the same time as the 205GTI. Citroën also adopted the GTI tag for the BX and CX high-performance variants.

A coupe for the future? The Griffe 4 design study from Peugeot's associates at Pininfarina was a 1985 idea of how a four-seater coupe version of the 205GTI could look.

205GTI — the numbers

Britain has become a major market for the Peugeot 205GTI, taking over 15% of the model's production from France. The production figures for the Cabriolet refer to both engine versions but the UK sales figures are for the CTI alone, as this is the only model offered.

	Production		UK registrations	
	GTI	**Cabriolet**	**GTI**	**CTI**
1984	35,437	—	1,874	—
1985	49,429	—	4,971	—
1986	45,917	5,872	7,378	427

Technical examination

The engineering behind this sharpest of hot hatchbacks analyzed by Jeffrey Daniels

JEFFREY DANIELS is a highly-respected technical writer of wide experience and interest, ranging from aeronautical to automotive engineering. He developed car testing techniques at *Motoring Which,* worked in management at the UK importers of Citroën and Datsun, and is now technical editor of *Autocar,* a post he held once before in the 1970s.

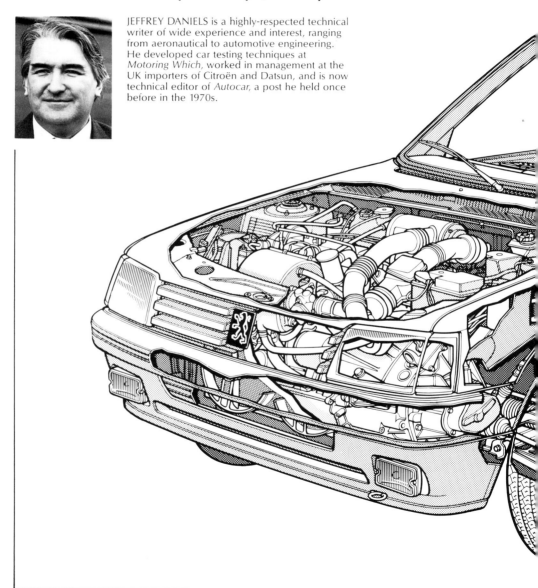

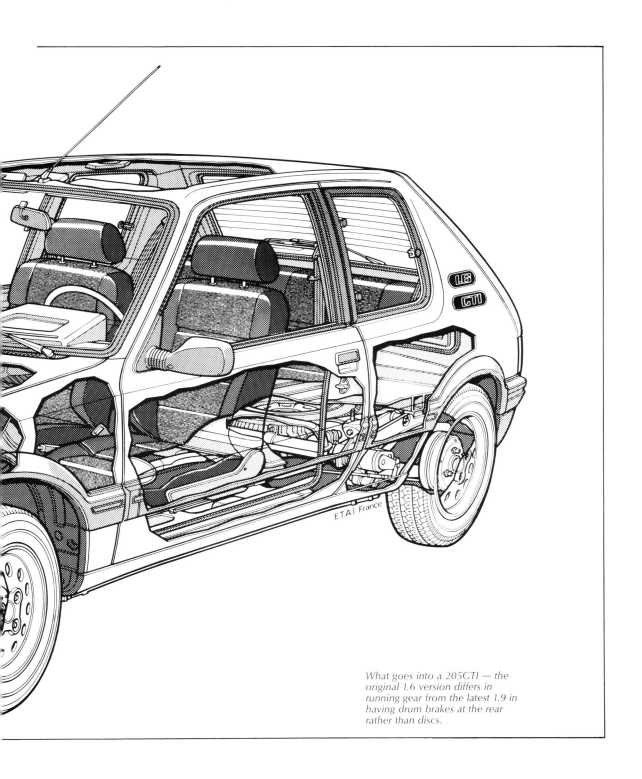

What goes into a 205GTI — the original 1.6 version differs in running gear from the latest 1.9 in having drum brakes at the rear rather than discs.

ETAI France

n a sense, the 205 GTI owes its origins to a diesel engine. But that is to leap several stages into the engineering story; the real starting point falls around 1972, when Peugeot launched the 104.

The 104 was an early example of the classic 'supermini' formula and it was a success, though hardly an emphatic one. It was always eclipsed by the original Renault 5 and for one reason: the Renault's styling was much the better. In mechanical terms the Peugeot had the edge, since it employed a brand-new, overhead-camshaft, all-alloy engine transversely installed, making the Renault's in-line, iron-blocked unit look old-fashioned — which indeed it was.

But the 104 proved a versatile design, its platform (in three different wheelbase lengths) also becoming the basis for the Citroën LN/LNA and Visa, and the Talbot Samba. The 104 itself appeared with several different power outputs, though always with some version of the rearward-inclined small 'Douvrin' XV/XW/XY-series engine under the bonnet. This light, efficient unit was progressively enlarged from its original 954cc to 1,360cc, developing up to 90bhp in highly-tuned, twin-carburettor versions.

What did surprise many observers was the absence of a diesel-engined 104, since Peugeot had been among Europe's pioneers of diesel passenger cars and the popularity of the diesel was surging in the mid-1970s aftermath of the oil embargo and energy crisis. In fact, the main problem was that the engine compartment of the 104 could not accommodate Peugeot's existing 'small' diesel, the engine used in the 204, 304 and 305. A diesel version of the 1,360cc Douvrin engine was designed and eventually shown in the VERA 02 research car in 1982, but it needed turbocharging to achieve an output of 62bhp, and the Peugeot product planners decided on an alternative approach.

Thus, when the team came to plan the Peugeot 205, successor to and replacement for the 104, there were at least two priorities. The first was to style a body that would have real visual impact: the design brief was essentially to come up with Peugeot's answer to the Renault 5. The second was that the new car must have an engine compartment big enough to accommodate a naturally-aspirated diesel engine powerful enough to give competitive performance.

The styling task was undertaken by Peugeot's own *Etudes et Recherches* department at La Garenne, under the direction of Gerard Welter. There was also a significant input from Pininfarina, Peugeot's long-established design consultant, and the tendency during development was for the teams to work in close harmony. Each would submit a styling proposal at various key stages of the process and the best features of both proposals would be combined and carried on to the next stage. The whole thing flew in the face of accepted convention, that all the best styling jobs are the unfettered expression of one mind, but there can be no quarrelling with the final result. The 205 as it eventually emerged — initially, in 1983, in five-door hatchback form only —

Compare the engine and transmission layout of the 205GT, above, with the XY8 engine inclined rearwards at 72 degrees with the gearbox beneath it, and the GTI, below, with the XU5 engine leaning forwards at 30 degrees with gearbox in line.

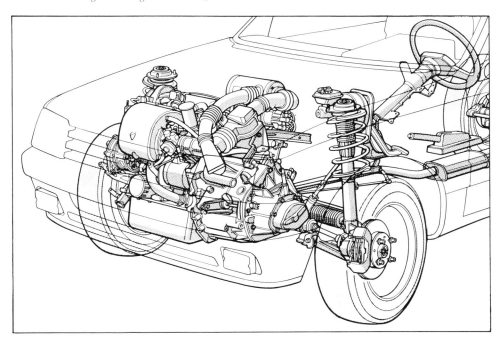

was undeniably pretty, aerodynamically efficient, well packaged and light but stiff. Also, there was enough room in the engine compartment for the required diesel engine.

That engine had already been seen. One of the corner-stones of PSA Peugeot-Citroën policy for the 1980s and beyond was that there should be a new 'corporate' medium-sized engine, optimized for low exhaust emissions and fully automated production, and adaptable to both petrol and diesel forms. This engine, the series XU, was in production at the new PSA Group facility at Metz-Tremery, where the latest techniques were employed in search of productivity, quality and reliability.

Unlike the small Douvrin engine, the XU was designed to drive through a gearbox in-line with the crankshaft, rather than beneath it. This eliminated the transfer-gear whine and rattle which had been a perpetual problem with the smaller unit in all its applications, but it made for a much wider package. That did not greatly matter in the medium-sized Citroën BX and Peugeot 305, which were the engine's first users (though the 305 nose structure had to be completely redesigned to get it to fit), but it called for some ingenuity on the part of the 205 design team.

However, to return to our opening line: it was the requirement to fit the 1,769cc XUD7 diesel engine in the 205, after early tests had shown this to be far superior to the alternative smaller diesel, which left the way open for the fitting of the dimensionally similar 1,580cc XU5 petrol version. And since it was possible, why not do it? Always provided, of course, that the chassis would cope with the demands of extra power and torque.

There was no real danger that the chassis would not be up to the task, for Peugeot has always been one of the world's 'class' chassis designers. Nor was the 205 to be a rebodied 104: the car was all-new, even though in some areas it resembled its predecessor. The wheelbase, for instance, remained the same as

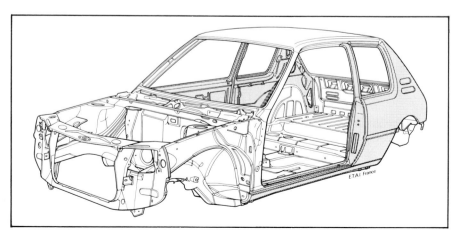

Shaded areas show the new body panels required to adapt the five-door 205 shell to the three-door configuration first used for the GTI.

Evolution of style — artist's rendering (above) shows early thinking on the 205's generic style, while the clay mock-up from April 1979 shows a shape close to the final product. Full-scale three-door models (below) are ideas considered at the design stage in 1978. Note that one has a much closer affinity to the 104 than the style eventually chosen.

one of the 104 variants at 242cm — just over 95in — but this is a logical choice for a small car which must sell on compact design for easy parking. Overall length was up by 3½in, accounted for entirely by the longer front overhang needed to make room for the XU engine, which was designed for installation leaning 30 degrees forwards compared with the 72 degrees rearward slant of the XV series. Necessity, however, was translated into a virtue by using the extra length to help smooth the nose into a much better aerodynamic shape: the standard 205's drag coefficient of 0.35 was highly competitive by 1983 standards.

The front suspension was still MacPherson strut, but it would have been strange for Peugeot of all people suddenly to abandon years of careful development and revert to double wishbones, especially in a design where weight control was very important. The rear suspension, too, remained as before in the sense that it used simple trailing arms — but its detail execution was completely different from that of the 104.

The real giveaway lay in certain other dimensions. The 205 was 3in wider in its front track than the 104, and 1in wider in rear track. One of the reasons for the extra width was, of course, the need to slot in the XU engine; but it also made for better stability and potentially better roadholding, allowing the same roll stiffness with softer spring and damper settings. Better, in fact: for the 205 was also 1in lower than the 104, and model for model it weighed some 100lb less. Such was the measure of the progress achieved in computer body stressing and advanced materials between 1970 and 1980.

While the front suspension was more or less typical of modern MacPherson-strutted designs, using offset springs and forged lower wishbones attached to a crossmember which also carried the steering rack and acted as a semi-subframe, the rear was new. Here the Peugeot 205's trailing arms were attached to crank-linkages, which transferred suspension loads not only to transverse torsion bar springs, but to dampers inclined close to the horizontal so that they would fit beneath the boot floor. The whole arrangement had been tested in the VERA research prototypes (and the rear damper system seen on the 305 estate car). It had proved effective in isolating the body from road rumble as well as easing maintenance problems and keeping the luggage space free of intruding turrets.

When the 205 appeared, all its petrol-engined versions used the XV/XW/XY-series Douvrin power units, so that the diesel was the only model with the XU engine. In view of the diesel's presence, not to mention Peugeot's simultaneous foray into top-class rallying with a turbocharged, four-wheel-drive 205 'silhouette' design, it was widely anticipated that the 205 would soon appear with the 1,580cc XU5 engine as fitted to the Citroën BX16 — a 94bhp engine with plenty of torque in the mid-range.

As a brand-new engine, the XU was full of development potential and 'stretch'. Its deceptively simple appearance belied the huge amount of work that had gone into its development. It was classically Peugeot in having an open-deck light-alloy block with pressed-in 'wet' cast-iron cylinder liners, located at their bottoms and held in place by the pressure of the light-alloy cylinder head (the diesel, by contrast, obtained its extra strength, stiffness and capacity through the use of a cast-iron block with siamesed cylinder bores, and a longer-stroke crankshaft).

In 1,580cc form, the XU5 was notably 'over-square', with a bore of 83mm and a stroke of 73mm. Its single belt-driven overhead camshaft bore directly on bucket-type tappets, the valves being in-line and the combustion chambers forming shallow 'bathtubs' matching shallow recesses in the pistons. The cylinder head design was crossflow, with the inlet manifold towards the front of the car. In 94bhp form in the Citroën BX, it ran a compression ratio of 9.5:1 and breathed through a twin-choke Weber carburettor. For the 205GTI, Peugeot's product planners had other ideas.

Above all, the planners were aware of the almost magical significance of the letter 'I' in the European market for fast small cars. It stands, of course, for (fuel)

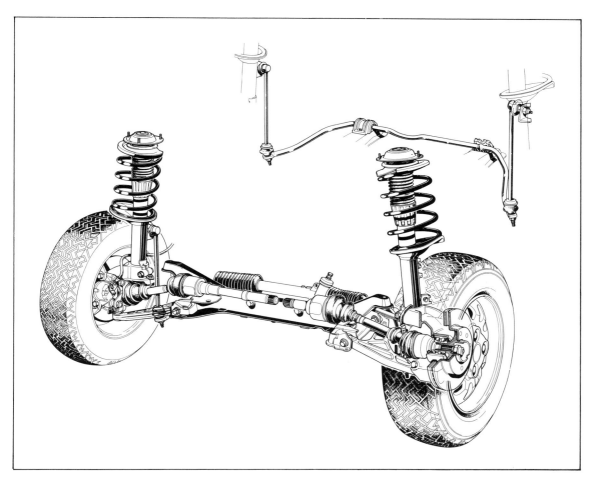

Front suspension is MacPherson strut with forged lower wishbones and anti-roll bar with cranked outer mountings.

Injection, though that had not stopped the builders of some competitors in the class — notably Alfasud — from labelling carburetted cars as 'ti'. Peugeot, however, was going to do the job properly, and even before the 205 appeared, the XU engine was well into development with a higher (10.2:1) compression ratio and Bosch L-Jetronic fuel injection. In this form, designated XU5J, the engine delivered 105bhp at 6,250rpm — quite enough to give the 205 a class-leading power-to-weight ratio. There was also an agreeably flat torque curve, thanks to modest valve timing with a total overlap of only 4 degrees, all the way from 2,700 to 5,500rpm, with a peak of 99lb/ft at 4,000rpm.

The Jetronic system was provided with fuel cut-off on the overrun down to 1,600rpm, but more significantly, this system was extended to provide a governor at 6,500rpm — a system much less easy to override than the former generation of centrifugally-parted points in the rotor arm! What is more, the governor was needed for long engine life, since without it the unit would run willingly and apparently without strain to 7,000rpm and beyond. Indeed, when an official 'works' tuning kit for the GTI was launched in 1985, the governor

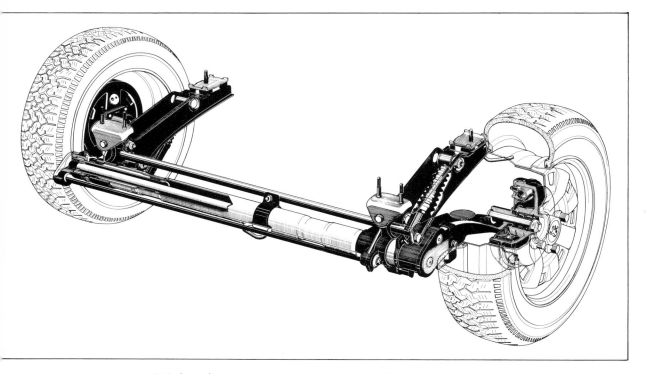

205 independent rear suspension is unusual, with trailing arms and transverse torsion bars and inclined dampers — in the interests of compactness below the load floor. Only the GT and GTI have a rear anti-roll bar.

software was deleted and users were simply advised not to exceed 7,000rpm — except for journalist road-testers, who were told they could safely but briefly go to 7,200rpm.

The rest of the 205 was equally thoroughly developed to make the most of its new-found power. The GTI was the first to use the three-door 205 body. Aerodynamics inevitably received attention, with a deeper front spoiler wide enough to mask the front wheels (and with shaped air ducts to the radiator) plus a new rear spoiler. The normal radiator grille was sealed, door surround sealing was improved and a streamlined driver's door mirror fitted. Together, these moves brought the drag coefficient down from 0.35 to 0.34 — an improvement well worth having in an acutely performance-conscious market, since it was worth 2-3mph in maximum speed.

The transmission was carefully matched to the engine characteristics. The gearbox was another PSA Group component, the BE1, with a close-spaced gear set. This was done in conjunction with a higher final-drive ratio than other 205s, though this still only gave 18.7mph per 1,000rpm in fifth gear. In other words, the GTI ran slightly over its power peak to 6,300rpm in reaching its claimed 118mph maximum speed. By early 1980s standards, this was deliberately sporting overall gearing for the sake of performance: any designer interested in ultimate economy and quietness would have chosen his overall gearing to give over 20mph per 1,000rpm, but the GTI was a model of relatively few compromises.

Suitable wheels, tyres and brakes had to be part of the GTI equation and — again taking the 205GT as the reference point — the tyres went from 165/70SR-13in to 185/60HR-14in, mounted on 5½J alloy instead of 5B steel rims. The front brake disc diameter remained the same, 9.7in, but the discs were now ventilated: even at the back, the width of the drum brakes was increased by a third to provide more rubbing surface, while the brake servo was increased from 7 to 9in diameter.

Though Peugeot planned a whole 'X' series of 205 three-doors to follow, the GTI was the pioneer and the simplification helped to hold down any weight increase caused by the performance modifications (the GTI scaled only 88lb more than the GT, yet the difference between the engine weights was rather more than that).

The steering ratio remained the same, giving an apparently leisurely 3.8 turns between locks for a strictly average 34ft turning circle, the latter partly dictated by the width of the engine/transmission package. But the Peugeot chassis engineers worked to take inertia out of the system and they modified the geometry to take account of the different wheel diameter and offset. Unlike some of its rivals, the 205GTI has never been criticized for vicious torque-steer. Inevitably, spring and damper rates were increased; some thought by too much, since the ride was one aspect of the early GTI which was criticized.

Since, by performance car standards, the XU5J engine in the 205GTI was still conservatively tuned, especially where valve timing was concerned, there was obvious scope for further development. Three main approaches were possible. The first and simplest was to redesign the camshaft to give greater overlap, but it transpired that this was not worth doing on its own. The inlet tracts for the L-Jetronic injection system had been carefully optimized for the original state of tune and any extra power achieved by the adoption of wilder valve timing on its own would have been far outweighed by the detrimental effect on fuel economy and exhaust emissions.

The second approach was to increase the valve lift and area, for which there was room. By improving the breathing while opening up the valve timing, gas speeds through the manifold were less affected. This combined approach was the basis first of the 1985 works tuning kit which offered a claimed 125bhp, and then, in mid-1986, of a Mark 2 revision of the production car. The revisions included the opening out of the inlet valves from 38.5 to 40.6mm diameter, for an 11% increase in valve area; the exhaust valves went from 31.5 to 33mm. Inlet valve lift was increased from 9.6 to 11.2mm and exhaust valve lift from 9.6 to

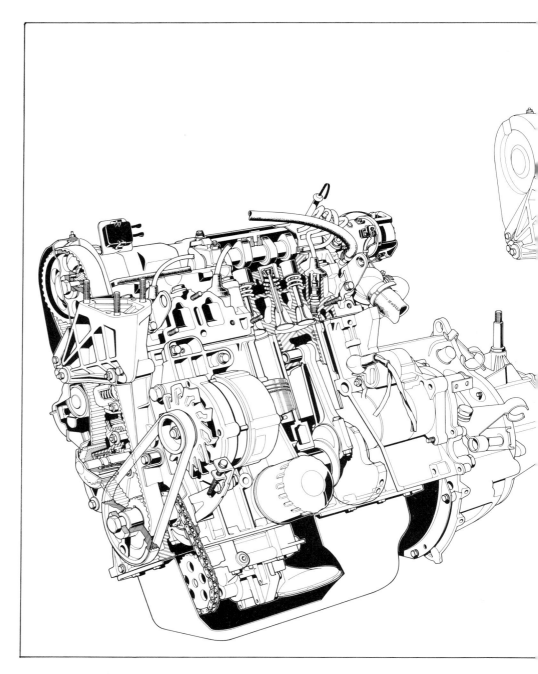

10.3mm. Total overlap in the new valve timing diagram was just under 11 degrees — still modest by most engine tuning standards.

The changes brought the output of the production 1.6-litre GTI to 115bhp, still at 6,250rpm, though there was a marginal (less than 1lb/ft) drop in torque, with the peak remaining at 4,000rpm. An interesting minor change was the lifting of the speed-governing fuel cut-off point to 6,900rpm. The penalties of engine tuning, even when carried out as thoroughly as this, could be seen in the

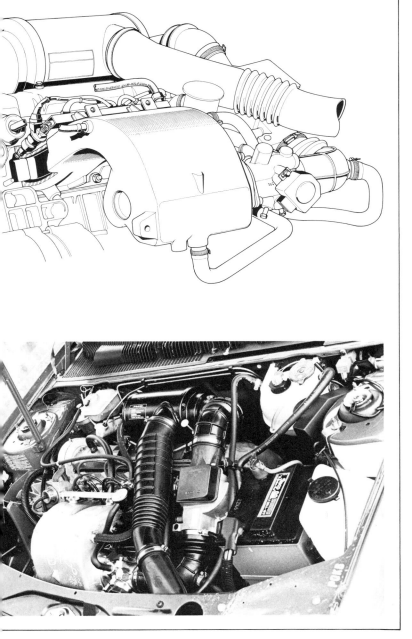

The XU5 engine is inclined forward, with the inlet manifold at the front of the engine compartment, though taking air via an air cleaner at its rear. Underbonnet photo shows the XU9JA of the GTI 1.9, which is of different internal dimensions but fundamentally the same engine as shown in the cutaway drawing.

steady-speed and urban fuel consumption figures, all of which were inferior by up to 5%; the comparison is valid, because the gearing remained unchanged, along with the other major features of the car.

While an extra 10bhp was well worth having, with a performance benefit which extended to 3mph higher top speed and nearly half a second off the 0-60mph time, the effect was more obvious at the top end of the performance scale. An all-round improvement really called for the third approach to engine development, namely to increase the capacity.

In theory, it was easy enough to open out the XU engine all the way to 1.9 litres: the XUD9 diesel version had been there from the outset. But there was more to it than taking the diesel block and crank and matching it to petrol injection components. The diesel, as already explained, had an integral cast-iron block, far stronger and heavier than the petrol engine needed. The diesel crank would likewise have been wasted on a petrol derivative. The alternative was to combine the linered upper end of the existing 1.6-litre petrol engine, retaining the 83mm bore, with a new crankshaft to take advantage of the space left in the basic design for the longer-throw diesel with its 15mm longer stroke (88 instead of 73mm).

Once again, the engine appeared in other PSA Group models, including the Peugeot 305GTX and the Citroën BX19GT, before being offered in the 205. And again, when it arrived to power a new version of the GTI, it had been fully developed into fuel-injected form.

The new engine, XU9JA, used the latest Bosch LE2 Jetronic injection and developed 130bhp at 6,000rpm. It retained the larger-diameter valves of the 115bhp 1.6-litre engine, but its camshaft had slightly more overlap, a total of just under 14 degrees. Extra 15bhp notwithstanding, the biggest benefit of the increased capacity was a peak torque of 119lb ft at 4,750rpm, with 108lb/ft (in other words, substantially more than the peak value for the 1.6-litre) available all the way from 2,200 to 6,000rpm.

The GTI chassis was modified in many details to cope with the extra output. First gear was raised, closing the ratio up towards the others but also, perhaps incidentally, reducing the peak torque it had to transmit; a new final drive ratio of 3.69:1 in conjunction with 185/55VR-15in tyres gave overall gearing of 20.9mph per 1,000rpm in fifth, still sufficiently low to take the engine just past peak power (to 6,100rpm) at the claimed 128mph maximum. The new tyres were fitted to 6J alloy rims of new design, with reduced offset. A revised front brake design with more efficient calipers resulted in a slight reduction of track, while that at the rear became wider by an equal amount with a change from drum to plain disc brakes. Wheel bearing diameters were substantially increased all round, a benefit of the larger wheel discs, and larger-diameter dampers completed the suspension picture.

In its 1.9-litre form — which runs in parallel with the 115bhp 1.6-litre version — the 205GTI has substantially better acceleration. Peugeot's claimed figures are better than 8sec to 60mph, and a standing quarter-mile covered within 16sec. Not surprisingly, though, the official steady-speed and urban fuel consumption figures show a further slight deterioration, even though they remain good by class standards.

In almost every respect, the Peugeot 205GTI looks like one of the very best developments of the front-driven, naturally-aspirated supermini concept.

While Peugeot knows a great deal about turbocharging — thanks to its Group B rally programme — the character of the GTI depends to some extent on its offer of the kind of instant, predictable engine response in any situation which even the best turbocars lack. No doubt the XU engine can and will sprout a four-valve head at some stage, but any significant improvement in the already excellent power-to-weight ratio of the 1.9-litre car will surely call for careful consideration of four-wheel drive. There again, Peugeot have learned so many valuable lessons from rallying...

Specifications

205GTI 1.6

Engine: Four-cylinder, in-line; aluminium block with replaceable liners, aluminium alloy cylinder head. Five main bearings. Single overhead camshaft driven by toothed belt. Bosch L-Jetronic fuel injection.

— 1984-1986 (Type XU5J 180A)
1,580cc, bore 83mm, stroke 73mm. Compression ratio 10.2:1. 105bhp (DIN) at 6,250rpm. 99lb/ft torque at 4,000rpm.

— 1986 onwards (Type XU5JA B6D)
1,580cc, bore 83mm, stroke 73mm. Compression ratio 9.8:1. 115bhp (DIN) at 6,250rpm. 98lb/ft torque at 4,000rpm.

Transmission
Five-speed, all indirect, with synchromesh.
Ratios (mph per 1,000rpm): 1st 3.31 (4.9); 2nd 1.88 (8.6); 3rd 1.36 (11.9); 4th 1.07 (15.2); 5th 0.87 (18.7). Final-drive ratio 4.06.

Suspension
Front: Independent, with MacPherson struts, coil springs, lower wishbones and anti-roll bar.
Rear: Independent, with trailing arms, transverse torsion bars, telescopic shock absorbers and anti-roll bar.

Steering
Rack and pinion, 3.8 turns from lock to lock.

Brakes
Front: 9.7in diameter ventilated discs. Rear: 7.1in diameter drums. Vacuum servo.

Wheels
5½J 14in diameter cast-alloy, with 185/60 HR radial-ply tyres. Tyre pressures, 29psi front and rear.

Capacities
Fuel tank: 11.0 gallons (50 litres).
Cooling system: 11.5 pints (6.5 litres).
Engine sump: 5 pints (2.85 litres).

Dimensions
Overall length: 145.9in. Overall width: 61.9in.
Overall height: 53.3in. Wheelbase: 95.3in.
Front track: 54.8in. Rear track: 52.3in.
Max payload: 937lb. Kerb weight: 1,874lb.

205GTI 1.9

Engine: Four-cylinder, in-line, aluminium block with replaceable liners, aluminium alloy cylinder head. Five main bearings. Single overhead camshaft driven by toothed belt. Bosch L-Jetronic fuel injection.
1,905cc, bore 83mm, stroke 88mm. Compression ratio 9.6:1. 130bhp (DIN) at 6,000rpm. 119lb/ft torque at 4,750rpm.

Transmission
Five-speed, all indirect, with synchromesh.
Ratios (mph per 1,000rpm): 1st 2.92 (6.2); 2nd 1.85 (9.8); 3rd 1.36 (13.3); 4th 1.07 (16.9); 5th 0.86 (20.9). Final-drive ratio 3.69.

Suspension
Front: Independent, with MacPherson struts, coil springs, lower wishbones and anti-roll bar.
Rear: Independent, with trailing arms, transverse torsion bars, telescopic shock absorbers and anti-roll bar.

Steering
Rack and pinion, 3.8 turns from lock to lock.

Brakes
Front: 9.7in diameter ventilated discs. Rear: 7.1in diameter solid discs. Vacuum servo.

Wheels
6J 15in diameter cast-alloy with 185/55 VR radial-ply tyres. Tyre pressures, 29psi front and rear.

Capacities
Fuel tank: 11.0 gallons (55 litres).
Cooling system: 11.6 pints (6.6 litres).
Engine sump: 8.8 pints (5.0 litres).

Dimensions
Overall length: 145.9in. Overall width: 61.9in.
Overall height: 53.3in. Wheelbase: 95.3in.
Front track: 54.4in. Rear track: 52.7in.
Max payload: 960lb. Kerb weight: 1,929lb.

Driving response

Kevin Blick's enthusiastic on-the-road assessment of the early 1.6 and the latest 1.9 205GTIs

Bigger does not always mean better. All too often the inevitable process of model development sees cars lose touch with their roots as they become too large, too luxurious or too powerful for their own good.

Happily, this hasn't happened to the Peugeot 205GTI. In its latest, 1.9-litre form, it is bigger-engined and considerably more powerful yet bursting with just the same exuberant, youthful energy that characterized the original car.

That is very good news, for the 205GTI has always been a car offering a subtle blend of virtues. To have turned it into a 130bhp hot-rod could have been a big mistake.

Indeed, the very essence of the 205GTI is 'small is beautiful'. When others, like the VW Golf GTI, were getting bigger and more expensive, the little 205 arrived and offered what looked like a return to the roots of the hot hatchback — small, simple, nimble and quick. When that first 1.6-litre, 105bhp 205GTI was launched, back in 1984, the market was already becoming crowded with hot hatchbacks; some a good deal hotter than others.

The new GTI wasn't claiming any performance records, but it stood out straight away. To begin with, it was pretty; among the drearily repetitive ranks of flashed-up family hatchbacks, the delicate curves of the diminutive Peugeot had a cheeky, chic appeal.

And it was fun to drive. Peugeot's publicity people clearly knew they were on to a winner by the confident way they launched the newcomer to Europe's Press. You can learn a lot on a car launch — or a little — depending on the nerve of the manufacturer and the type and length of route they choose for the test run. Peugeot just pointed us in the right direction across 120 miles of twisting, mountainous southern Spain and left us to find out the rest...

KEVIN BLICK was road test editor of *Autocar* before becoming editor of the monthly magazine *What Car?* and is now a freelance writer, specializing in car testing. At one time a keen amateur rally driver, he has used a 205GTI for two years as part of the long-term test programme of *Fast Lane* magazine.

At speed there is little to distinguish the 1.9 from the lower-powered versions. Frontal aspect is the same, so, more importantly, is the high standard of handling and stability.

What I found was an exciting, exuberant little machine; utterly responsive and perfectly at home on the sinuous climbs and descents. A few months afterwards I began a long-term test of a 205GTI for *Fast Lane* magazine; two years and 24,000 miles later I hadn't found anything to make me change that initial judgment.

Responsive. That's the word which keeps coming back to describe that GTI and others since, including the 1.9. Responsive in performance and responsive in handling. The original 105bhp version of the GTI used, as you've read elsewhere, a new Bosch-injected, 1,580cc version of PSA's corporate XU engine. A clean, quick-revving engine, the all-alloy unit is one of the nicest in its class, even if it does not quite have the smoothness of, say, a Golf. What it shares with the German car, however, is a superb breadth of worthwhile torque — 90% of peak torque being available across a 3,000rpm band.

That was a characteristic retained when Peugeot uprated the engine to 115bhp by enlarging the valves and altering the timing. This current 1.6-litre combines the hefty torque of its predecessor with an ability to rev through the red line to a 6,900rpm ignition cut-out — the 105bhp model stopped at 6,500rpm.

Given the power of the latest 1,905cc XU9 engine and low weight of the little 205, it was obvious that the GTI 1.9 could scarcely fail to inherit the 'responsiveness' gene. And of course it does, even if peak torque is developed at a surprisingly high 4,750rpm. (By way of compensation, around 80% of this figure is available all the way from 2,000 to 6,000rpm.)

The big engine does not quite have the same eager, free-revving style as junior, but it is still smooth and unlaboured, and with such ample reserves of punch, it really doesn't need to be worked hard. Its flexibility is tremendous; it will pull with ease from below 2,000rpm and, more significantly, make the jump between 50 and 70mph (or any other intermediate check) with leonine power. Rarely was the case for a large-capacity conventional engine better argued against those who advocate four-valve cylinder heads or turbocharging as alternative routes to similar performance.

Some prestigious rivals find themselves stumbling embarrassingly behind the GTI 1.9 in this important mid-range acceleration — more critical to everyday performance than the usually quoted 0-60mph data. Not that the GTI 1.9 is short of straight-line speed — it is well capable of ducking under the 8-second barrier for the 0-60mph test track dash.

What really sets the seal on both GTIs' performance are their perfectly-chosen sets of gear ratios. Unlike some, Peugeot didn't skimp on

Not much body roll when cornering fast, as this rear shot shows. Also apparent is the good all-round visibility through the deep front and rear screens.

The driving position is good for most sizes of driver, though the steering column is not adjustable. After complaints from owners, the wheel rim was changed from mock to real leather for 1987 model year.

The central console, including pop-out ashtray and digital clock, is not the neatest piece of design. The heater/ventilator controls are alongside and the hazard warning, heated rear window and rear fog lamp push switches are above.

The GTI seats are a special shape and have unique cloth covering. Nylon material and seat back 'suspension' do tend to show signs of wear. When launched in France, the 1.9-litre version was offered with either cloth (to a new design) or leather-sided seats; for the UK, the leather-trimmed version (right) became standard.

important but costly development details, and lowered the top three ratios of the standard BE1 'box to produce a set of low, close gears that are an enthusiast's delight.

Accelerate hard through the gears, which change with the lightest flick-flick of the deliciously short, accurate shift, and the power just keeps on flowing — right on up to the fifth-gear rev-limiter in the 1.6 model and past 6,000rpm in the higher-geared 1.9. That's enough to turn both into genuine 120mph-plus cars. Combine those ratios with that torque spread and 'responsive' becomes an understatement for the GTI's performance; like an eager racehorse, it is always just asking to be given its head.

One might have expected the downside of such performance to be an over-eagerness for fuel, but both versions of the GTI normally keep this situation well under control. They have to be driven very hard indeed before economy starts to drop a long way below 30mpg.

The Bosch electronic fuel injection that does so much for this economy also gives both engines a reassuring consistency of performance. They start instantly at the twist of a key, hot or cold, and never falter or fluff.

It isn't just the GTI's performance that deserves praise; its handling is eager and responsive, too. Too eager and responsive for some, it has to be admitted, though I'm not among them.

Short in wheelbase and wide in track, the little GTI has the basic characteristics to be a reactive machine and Peugeot hasn't tried to conceal them. Body roll has been tightly constrained, while the steering is quick and sharp. The result is a car which couldn't be happier than on a twisting country road. It's nimble, agile and exciting. With that instant, responsive engine, the quick steering and roll-free cornering, it almost seems to come alive on a secondary road.

But though the car is so alert to quick movements of the wheel, giving it a delightfully sharp turn-in to any bend, steering effort does build up noticeably with cornering force. The steering is heavy at parking speeds, too, making the GTI disproportionately hard work to manoeuvre for a car of its size. Indeed, some drivers believe the increased steering load is a sign that the car is near its cornering limits. Not so; heave the wheel harder and you'll be startled at the reserves of grip. It really is very difficult to unstick at the front.

On the other hand, the ease with which the rear end of early models lost grip if a driver backed off the throttle caused much comment. I liked it, finding the fail-safe handling of most front-wheel-drive hot hatches just a little uninspiring. The tail of current models doesn't whip quite so readily out of line, though once it does go it does so quickly and has to be gathered up smartly. Though a little less of a rally-racer than it was at first, the present balance is probably just about right, for there is still a lot of fun to be had. It is still a highly-strung little car — very much the lion cub of the Peugeot range; boisterous and playful.

One doesn't need to rev the engine fiercely or corner at the limit to appreciate the eager appeal of the GTI: one of its charms is that it is a lively, agile and enjoyable little machine at almost any speed. I haven't talked separately of the two GTI versions. They are, in fact, very similar in their driving style. The bigger car needs more care; its power and torque are pushing at the limits of the 205's chassis, as one notices when scrabbling on a tight corner or accelerating from a standstill, but then it does run on the same 185-section tyres as the 1.6, though with a lower 55, rather than 60, profile. The 1.9 also uses disc rear brakes where the other has drums, though both have a solid, reassuring pedal with a progressive action.

At the same time as the early GTI's handling was amended, so a more serious deficiency, its ride, was dealt with. Don't believe that the first GTIs had an altogether bad ride; in fact they had a good ride on bad roads, but a bad ride on good roads! Small wheel movements provoked an uncomfortable bouncing, which could go on for mile after mile on a mildly bumpy motorway — very unpleasant. That is now a thing of the past, and both 1.6 and 1.9 versions ride very well by the standards of sporting cars. Naturally, there is clattering and jarring over low-speed, city-centre potholes, especially with the lower-profiled tyres of the 1.9, but otherwise only a very occasional trace of that bounciness.

If all the pleasures of the GTI centre around it being a small, responsive machine, then it's only fair that its shortcomings should be the product of its basic size, too. It is, after all, a small car — derived from a supermini rather than a medium hatchback, like so many rivals. So it is not only smaller inside than cars like the Golf GTI or Escort XR3i, but also more skimpy. The trim is simple and, despite improvements, cheap; more areas of painted metal show than in the classier but much more costly Golf, the doors shut with a hollow clang, and the column stalks work with a noisy click-clack.

The facia wouldn't win any design awards. A comprehensive pack of six small instruments is squeezed into the 205's binnacle, but the switchgear is scattered along the dash. Heater slides on the centre console are tricky to use accurately and, disappointingly, the GTI, like the rest of the 205 range, has an unsophisticated heating system with no separate ventilation.

On the positive side, there are two big, grippy front bucket seats which give exactly the sort of support needed in this car against cornering loads. And the GTI 1.9 has smarter leather side panels, as well as a leather covering for its fat-rimmed steering wheel. It has other luxurious additions, too, in the shape of central locking, electric windows and air horns.

Neat detail — the interior light unit (left) at roof centre behind the screen rail is a PSA corporate fitment and includes a conventional interior light and swivelling map spot lamp automatically turned on when flicked left or right. Electric windows (right) — standard on 1.9 — have switches built into the front door pockets, two on the driver's side, one for the passenger. Central locking comes with electric windows as an option package on the 1.6 model.

The 205GTI being given its head on a twisting road — 'sheer good fun' says author Blick.

There is more room in the back seat of the GTI than one might have anticipated — but then the 205 is one of the biggest cars in the supermini class — and the boot, which has the bonus of 50/50 split-fold rear seat backs, can carry a decent load.

The 205GTI is a car of a very strong character. If you own one, there are times undoubtedly when you will tire of it. On a long run, the relatively low gearing means that engine buzz is ever present, along with a background hubbub of wind and road roar. In time, they all seem to develop rattles and creaks. And, being so responsive, it's a car that has to be driven with concentration all the time, for it can be unforgiving of mistakes.

Yet take it to a twisting country lane and you'll fall in love with it all over again. I test a lot of cars, but I have yet to drive one which matches the sheer good fun of the GTI down my favourite stretch of secondary road. And that, after all, is what a car like this is all about.

Performance

The 205GTI has been widely praised in road tests published throughout Europe. In Britain, the definitive tests are those carried out by the weekly magazines *Autocar* and *Motor* and these figures are published with the kind permission of their respective Editors:

	1.6 GTI (105bhp)		1.6 GTI (115bhp)	CTI	1.9 GTI	
	Autocar	*Motor*	*Autocar*	*Autocar*	*Autocar*	*Motor*
Max. speed	116	117	122	116	120	123
0-30mph	2.9	3.1	3.1	3.0	2.9	3.1
0-40mph	4.5	4.6	4.7	4.7	4.1	4.5
0-50mph	6.2	6.4	6.5	6.5	5.9	6.0
0-60mph	8.6	8.7	8.7	8.9	7.8	7.7
0-70mph	11.4	11.5	11.3	11.8	10.8	10.7
0-80mph	15.2	15.3	14.8	15.6	13.7	13.6
0-90mph	20.2	20.6	19.5	20.8	18.2	17.8
0-100mph	29.5	27.5	26.6	29.7	23.8	23.0
Standing $\frac{1}{4}$-mile	16.6	16.8	17.4	17.5	16.3	16.4
Standing kilometre	30.9	30.9	31.1	31.7	30.2	29.9
Overall mpg	29.5	31.3	29.9	30.7	28.1	27.8

Open and shut case

The 205CTI, a close relative of the GTI, is for fresh air fans. How the Cabriolet came about and what it is like to drive described by Ray Hutton

Peugeot may not have produced very sporting cars before the advent of the 205GTI, but they did keep faith with the convertible. While, until the 1980s, most manufacturers had rejected open cars as uneconomic to build, Peugeot continued with their 204, 304 and 504 Cabriolets. In 1982, one of the steps taken to enliven the Talbot image was to introduce a convertible version of the little Samba. Its body was developed and produced by Pininfarina in Turin.

So, as the 205 evolved, a convertible was an obvious addition to the range. And, since the Samba exercise had shown the advantage of having the 'irregular' parts of a low-volume model made away from the main production lines, Peugeot once again called upon their long-time associates in Italy.

It is not perhaps widely recognized that as well as being one of the leading automotive design consultancies, Pininfarina also have the capacity to make some 30,000 cars a year. Their output ranges from the Ferrari Testarossa and Cadillac Allante to the two-seater Alfa Romeo Spider. In most cases they are responsible for building, painting and trimming the bodies, which are then transported to the client's factory for the installation of the mechanical parts.

For the 205 Cabriolet, some three-door body parts are supplied from Mulhouse and Sochaux to Pininfarina's Grugliasco plant, where the convertible body is built, corrosion-protected and painted. It is then fitted with its hood and the trim parts that are exclusive to the convertible, before being shipped back to Mulhouse for final assembly alongside the fixed-roof 205s.

While the styling of the original 205, and the GTI version, was done in the Peugeot studio using many of Pininfarina's ideas, the design adaptation to

RAY HUTTON writes about cars and the motor business for the *Sunday Express Magazine, The Observer Magazine* and a number of motor trade and industry publications in the UK as well as the American magazine *Car and Driver.* Previously editor of *Autocar,* Ray, a satisfied 205GTI owner for two years, is also the editor of this MRP Enthusiast's Companion.

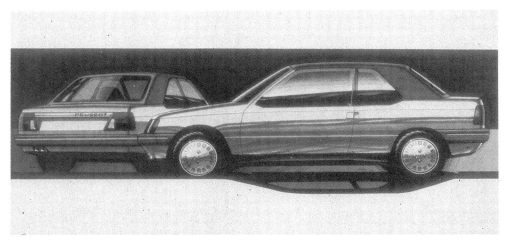

Pininfarina designed and produce the 205 Cabriolet. The styling drawings, (opposite), show how the shape developed, while in the Grugliasco factory, (above), bodies are built up, trimmed, and then transported back to France for final assembly.

produce the Cabriolet was carried out entirely in Turin. Discussions started in May 1983 and by January 1984 the design had been finalized and construction of 11 prototypes commenced. Production started, gently at first, in September 1985, though the car did not go on sale until the following spring.

The prototypes went through an extensive rough-road test programme for, as Peugeot and Pininfarina know better than most, making a convertible out of a modern saloon is a deceptively complex business. Today's computer techniques enable designers to produce lightweight body/chassis that are stiff and strong, but they depend on the roof for much of that rigidity. Take the top off, even replacing it with a stout roll-over bar, and, inevitably, much of the torsional stiffness disappears.

So under the skin of the 205 Cabriolet are some major changes intended to make good that loss. The platform has two new cross-members, one of which supports the stout roll bar; there is a further, tubular roll-over hoop within the windscreen frame; and the side sills have been increased in cross-section and actually protrude rather more under the doors (though this is scarcely noticeable). The doors are modified from the standard items supplied from France; the windows are frameless, and the Cabriolet has quarter-lights that the ordinary 205 lacks. And, because the original is a hatchback, new side panels and boot lid had to be devised.

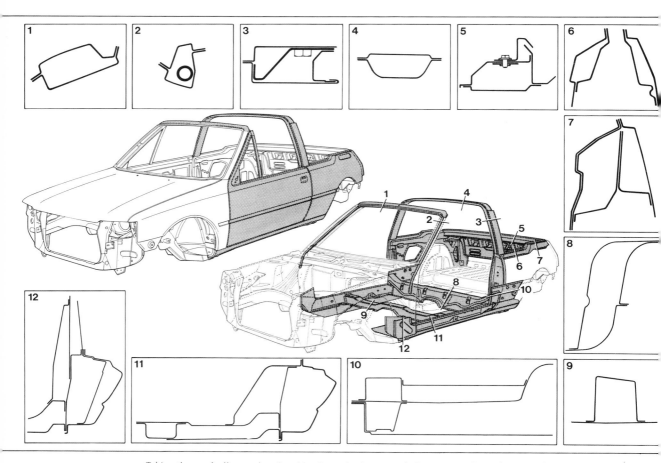

Taking the roof off a modern hatchback is a far from simple business as these drawings showing the unique panels and body under-parts of the Cabriolet confirm. The numbered cross-sections reveal the complexity of some of the structural members.

The result is a bodyshell which, according to Pininfarina's research and development chief Leonardo Fioravanti, is about 90lb heavier than the three-door saloon. Peugeot's figures, comparing similar specifications, show that the whole car is 188lb heavier — most of the additional weight being accounted for by the hood structure.

In France, the 205 Cabriolet was launched in two versions, the CT and CTI, with the 80bhp 205GT and 115bhp 205GTI engines. With production limited and a relatively high price, Peugeot decided only to offer the higher specification in the UK.

The CTI is mechanically identical to the 1.6-litre GTI. Because it is heavier, it is about $\frac{1}{2}$sec slower to accelerate to 60mph and inferior aerodynamics reduce its maximum speed by 5mph. The suspension is softer, too, but not by much.

*Open-air sports —
thanks to the integral
roll-over bar and
extensive efforts made
to preserve the GTI's
characteristics in the
open version, the CTI is
a much less hazardous
proposition than hang
gliding!*

*View from the back. The
roll-over bar is not too
obtrusive and the rear
seat accommodation
remains as good as in
the saloon — but at
speed, occupants have
a windy ride.*

*Pininfarina had to do
extensive restyling at the
back to devise a
conventional boot lid
and keep the folded
hood 'rump' as low as
possible.*

Most of the time the CTI has the same crisp response as the GTI, but some kinds of undulating roads make it 'wriggle' and the accompanying scuttle shake signals that, despite all its makers' efforts, it does not have as rigid a body as the saloon.

This is a minor matter for those who crave open-air motoring, and the 205CTI makes that both convenient and fun. Up to a point. These drophead conversions are not for serious high-speed motoring with the hood down, though the Peugeot is better than most. At 100mph on the *autobahn*, wind noise and buffetting are unpleasant enough to make the most avid fresh-air driver stop to put the roof up.

Pininfarina have done their best to reduce these effects. They have put their wind tunnel to use in refining the Cabriolet's shape and the wind protection it provides with the hood down. The big quarter-lights and the wrap-over windscreen header rail certainly help, and at more modest speeds — and certainly for shorter drivers who sit lower and closer to the screen — it is more comfortable riding top-down in the Peugeot than in its convertible competitors.

The CTI's hood is well-made and easy to put up or drop down. It is made of PVC on a cotton backing and is fully lined in a material called Teppelux, with insulated padding. Two gas struts within the rear quarters make it light to handle and there are only two screen-rail latches — massive handle-cum-hooks — to deal with. No great effort is involved and one person can quickly open or close the top. The operation is easier with the doors open and the windows down, and care must be taken to avoid trapping the radio aerial, mounted on the screen rail, when refitting the hood.

Designers have a conflict between space for the folded hood and room for luggage, which is why the CTI, like its convertible rivals, has a 'rump' which does restrict over-the-shoulder visibility to some extent. Stowage — and the desire for wide rear vision with the hood in place — dictated the use of flexible plastic for the good-sized rear window. This can't be heated like a glass one and undeniably represents a greater security risk. On the plus side, it can easily be zipped out for added ventilation — or replacement, should it become scratched or damaged.

With the hood up, at town speeds, driver and front seat passenger would scarcely realize that they were in a convertible. At 70mph or more, wind noise is considerably higher, but otherwise the closed CTI has all the comforts and qualities of the hatchback. There is still plenty of room in the back as well, and the 'basket handle' roll bar that doubles as a hood support, window runner and seat belt mounting, is not too obtrusive. The rear side windows, of rather different shape to the hinged ones of the hatchback, wind down about 6 inches.

The stowed hood does not take away any of the luggage space, which

Though it is a weighty structure, cleverly arranged hinging and gas-strut assistance make light of folding the hood. It takes only moments, requiring only the release of the two handles at the screen rail and some attention to careful folding of the flexible plastic rear window. The folded hood is not very tidy, though, and needs the tonneau cover, which can be a tight fit (below). Press studs are used outside, Velcro strip behind the seats to secure the inside — rather a fiddle.

though rather small is well-shaped and easily stowed via a full-width boot lid. The rear seat retains the 50/50 split of the hatch so that the luggage area can be extended; the seats can only be folded forward after releasing a catch in the boot. A tonneau cover is supplied to cover the hood rump and once fitted is flap-free, but with its rigid side pieces it is a rather awkward thing to carry around.

The 205CTI has proved a most successful addition to the range. It replaced the Samba Cabriolet in the Peugeot model line-up. In its first year, 1986, nearly 6,000 205 Cabriolets were made and production was to be expanded to 7,500 for 1987.

Keeping in shape

Stuart Bladon provides tips on how to get the best out of your 205GTI — new or old

A dvice from engineers used to working on the 205GTI is that owners should not attempt to do more than basic maintenance on this car. Paid mechanics have a natural loathing of anyone else trying to do their work for them; but in this case it seems there is justification for the caution, on account of the special tools and equipment needed for much of the work. But there is still much about the GTI and CTI that the owner could usefully know, even if he does not propose to get his hands dirty under the bonnet.

A prime example of this is the fuel injection system, which cannot be set up properly without aid of a CO meter. For this reason, adjusters on the butterflies and mixture control are sealed and not to be disturbed by the well-intended home mechanic who would dearly love to set it up by ear.

Despite this caution, 'emergency action' can be taken over the slow-running speed, which may sometimes prove necessary when the fuel-flow cut-off valve, which operates on the over-run, gets slightly out of adjustment. Late re-opening of the valve can result in stalling, but this may be temporarily eased by speeding up the idling rpm. Under the bonnet, close to the bonnet catch, will be seen a brass screw which regulates the tickover; but bear in mind that adjusting idling speed may upset the mixture, which will need to be reset subsequently using a CO meter. The cause of the problem — incorrect setting of the over-run shut-off valve — also needs to be rectified with the necessary workshop equipment.

Turning the slow-running screw in (clockwise as viewed from the front) reduces idling speed, and anti-clockwise rotation increases it. Slacken the lock-nut on the lower end of the screw before and after adjustment, and do not attempt to change slow-running speed too much. If it is badly out, some other more positive cause is indicated.

There are two versions of the 1.6-litre engine, with power outputs of 105 and

STUART BLADON spent the first 26 years of his career in motoring journalism on the staff of *Autocar* and now contributes regularly to a number of motoring magazines and writes twice-weekly reports on ITV Oracle. He has always enjoyed the practical side of car ownership and does most of the servicing on his own 205.

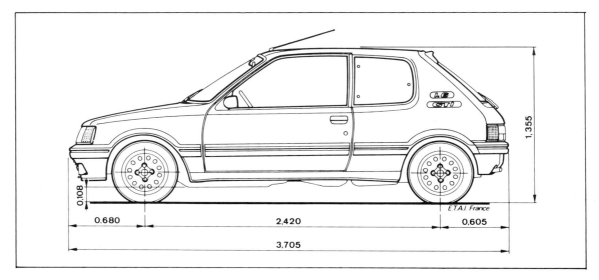

205 GTI dimensional drawing shows measurements in millimetres.

115bhp respectively; and while in the area of the injection system it is worth knowing that a breather pipe running forward from the oil filler to the injection manifold reveals that the more powerful unit is fitted. The chassis number after which the 115bhp engine was fitted is 7330000, but there were some before then. A more positive identification is the engine number type: 105bhp is XU5J 180A; 105bhp, XU5JA B6D.

In May 1986, a change of fuel pump was made towards the end of the G series of chassis numbers in a bid to reduce noise. The change proved unsatisfactory, and Peugeot reverted to the original pump, and the 800-odd cars involved were converted. In about 90% of cases, conversion was done before sale, and the number involved in recall was very small.

A fairly straightforward task which the owner can undertake is the interim service, involving renewal of engine oil and filter. Oil changes are always best done after a run, while the oil is still hot and any impurities well dispersed; but don't go underneath armed with a big adjustable spanner! The Peugeot 205 (all models) has a sump plug with recessed square aperture for which a tool with 8mm shank is needed. This is available from Peugeot dealers. Take care not to lose the copper washer.

At the same time as the oil is changed (every 6,000 miles), the filter should be renewed. Unless you have Herculaean grip, you will not be able to do it by hand, and must be armed with a strap wrench of the kind which can be wrapped round the filter and is pulled tight by the action of hauling on the lever. Access for this is not good, and it should be tackled from underneath, taking care not to damage the radiator. When removing the filter, ensure that the

The underbonnet is crowded, though the reservoirs — brake fluid, radiator header tank and screen washer — are accessible. Checking and replenishment of oil is not all that easy; the dipstick handle nestles between the intake trunking towards the rear of the engine, while the filler is to the right of the intake plenum chamber. The breather pipe connecting the oil filler to the injection manifold identifies the 115bhp 1.6 model, (centre picture). Otherwise there are few changes from the 105bhp original, (upper picture) The latest 1.9-litre model (lower picture) also has little to identify it in the engine compartment; compare with the two 1.6 variants

rubber seal is not left behind; a new seal comes with the replacement filter.

If undertaking this interim service yourself, be sure to carry out the rest of the routine and not just sign off with changing the oil and filter. The full 6,000-mile service calls for a check on brake fluid reservoir, cooling system, windscreen washer reservoirs, tyre pressures, all lights and turn indicators, and visual inspection of pipes and hoses for signs of leakage. Do not omit the rear brake flexible pipes.

Usually, a low-maintenance battery will be fitted, requiring no attention, but if not, check electrolyte level. Every two years, the coolant should be flushed out and anti-freeze renewed; and good quality anti-freeze must be in the system year round — never plain water.

Another small job which the owner-mechanic can do is replacement of the fuel filter, located on the firewall. It's a straightforward task, but is required only every 48,000 miles. If you *do* change it, make sure the dealer is informed, or he will do it again at that service! Every 24,000 miles, the paper air cleaner filament should be changed — another simple task which can be done by the enthusiast to help cut servicing costs.

From time to time it is sensible to check the tightness of the short longitudinally-grooved alternator drive belt. It needs to be *very* tight — not like the old days of looking for $\frac{3}{4}$in of slack at the mid-point between pulleys; if yours is like that, the alternator probably will not be charging adequately. The easiest way to check for tightness of this drive belt is to try to turn the alternator fan by hand. If you can just move it with difficulty, it is probably about right. If it can be pushed round fairly easily, then it's too loose, and adjustment is needed. Slacken the lock nut beneath the screw adjuster at the front of the alternator, turn the threaded bolt until the tension is judged to be right, and retighten the locking bolt.

After the winter, it's a good idea to check that the thermostatically controlled cooling fan is working properly. It could have gone wrong at the beginning of the winter and with the lower ambient temperatures prevailing, its absence might not be a problem. Simply check that the fan cuts in after the engine has been left ticking over a few minutes. There are two speeds for the cooling fan, normal speed being reduced by a resistance, which is by-passed if the engine gets very hot and extra cooling is needed. The resistance is located at the left of the engine bay (right as you face it), near the firewall; be careful not to touch it after the fan has been running as it gets very hot.

Surprisingly, there is no way of checking the oil level in the gearbox and final drive, the level being established by the 'drain and insert measured quantity' technique. Earlier models have separate drain plugs for gearbox and differential; later, they went to one common drain point. Even the earlier models with two drain plugs have only one filler, located on the side of the gearbox casing. Make sure that you have removed the correct plug, and after

Access to the GTI's surprisingly generous rear compartment is made easier by the cranked hinge arrangement which tips the whole seat rather than just the seat back. The release lever at the back of the cushion needs to be positively re-engaged, otherwise passengers can have the shock of the seat clicking into place when the car accelerates!

refitting drain plugs, pour in $3\frac{1}{2}$ pints, using a dispenser such as the type supplied by Castrol with their oil. Be careful not to spill any, or you will lose track of the measurement and not know how much more to pour in. Incidentally, one of the engineers who briefed me on the 205GTI advised that $3\frac{1}{2}$ pints should be put into all models, even if the book says $2\frac{1}{2}$. Internally, it spills over from the gearbox into the differential sump.

Being fully electronic, the distributor needs no attention, but timing may require verification. There is no static check on timing; it can be done only with a strobe, and requires an assistant to hold the engine at 3,000rpm. Advance should be 30 degrees at this speed, with the vacuum pipe to the distributor disconnected. The timing mark is rather buried away behind all the fuel injection pipework and manifold, and should be cleaned before starting the test. To rectify any timing error, slacken the distributor clamp bolts, and rotate the distributor with a hand protected by a thick glove or other insulator. Check again after retightening, and remember to reconnect the vacuum pipe for the advance/retard.

Rear seats are split 50:50, cushions are pulled forward by loops and then backs fold forward after levers are released. Rear seat belts, standard for 1987, have reels concealed below the side supports of the parcel shelf.

Maximum load area, with both halves of the rear seat folded forward and the parcel shelf removed. The extended floor is more-or-less flat and has a fairly durable plastic covering.

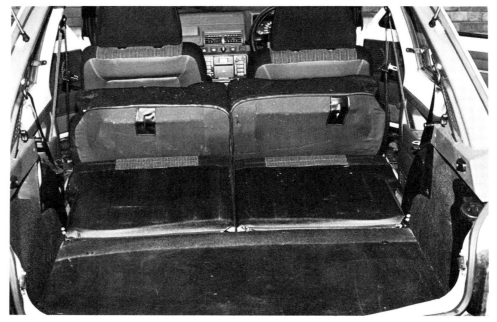

Valve clearance adjustment is a big job, since the gaps have to be measured first, then the camshaft removed, and shims under the buckets exchanged for ones of the required thickness. It is a long and fiddly job, but one not likely to be needed until after an extended mileage. It would normally be done as routine after cylinder head attention.

Difficulty in changing gear may be experienced, and is usually due not so much to any fault in the gear selectors as to failure of the clutch to free properly when the pedal is depressed. The clutch is cable-operated, and adjustment is made at the clutch end. It is a job to be tackled from underneath, and after the locknut — situated near the gearbox filler plug — has been slackened, the cable is adjusted until the pedal is level with the brake pedal.

It will be noted that there is an earthing strap from the top of the MacPherson strut each side. As well as eliminating static, this is important for the disc brake pad warning light.

As we leave the engine area, an important point to be remembered is always to close the bonnet by letting it drop from a height of about 18in. Never push it down, which can cause dents in the panel.

Also to be noted in the engine bay is the location of the jack and wheelnut spanner. A little rehearsal of wheel-changing technique on a sunny Sunday afternoon saves time and anguish for when you have to 'do it for real', in the dark and the rain, while dressed for dinner. The spare wheel, carried on a wind-down trestle under the boot floor, is exposed to the worst of winter's muddy and salty roads, and it is a good idea to take it out from time to time for inspection, pressure check and cleaning. Some take the precaution of wrapping it before stowing it away again, but make sure that the wrapping is

Early GTIs did not have a separate reservoir for the rear window washer and fluid therefore took a long time to reach its destination. Later models have this rear window washer bottle to the boot side.

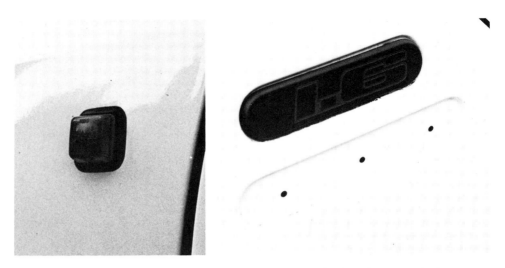

(Left) Identification point of post-1986 models are the side repeaters for the indicators on the front wings just forward of the doors. GTI side badges (right) all too often disappear, as they are easily levered off. A suggested solution is to apply a touch of strong adhesive around the push-fasteners.

waterproof. If the wheel lives in a soggy mess, never able to dry out, it will suffer more than just slung as the makers intended it to be.

Two kinds of disc brake are used, with different pad location — one uses a wedge and clip, the other the more usual system of two retaining pins with security clips. Note carefully the arrangement before dismantling, and pads can then easily be removed and new ones fitted. If a trace of brake squeal has been present, fitting new pads may cure it, for a while at least, as all now have an abrasive surface, which scrubs the discs in the first few applications. For this reason, brakes should be used rather gently for a while after fitting new pads.

Front disc brakes are, of course, internally vented on all models, and the 1.9 has discs at the rear as well as the front (solid for the rear). Renewing front discs is easy — just two Philips screws to be undone and the disc drops on the floor. All the work of location is done by the wheel bolts. The rear drum brakes are not so simple as they are in unit with the wheel bearing. No puller is needed, but a special spanner is necessary to undo the securing nut. The bearing has to be resecured to the correct tightness, and the recommendation is that rear brake attention is a 'dealer job'.

It used not to be possible to renew the rear wheel bearing without also changing the drum, but now the bearing is obtainable without having to buy a new drum as well.

Incidentally, most GTIs develop a disturbing groaning when braking in reverse; it isn't anything to worry about, but neither is it easily cured. Generally, knocks and squeaks need to be investigated, as they are often the portent of something going wrong. Knocks at the front end, during hard cornering, may be traced to no more than one of the sub-frame bolts which has worked slightly loose. Rear suspension is by transverse torsion bars which are 'handed' with a degree of preliminary twist. In cases of rear suspension squeak, a technique to remedy this is to drill the main transverse tube which locates the whole suspension, squirt in a quarter of a pint of oil, fit a plug, and then drive violently round two or three corners to spread the oil!

Rear dampers have been known to fail fairly early, and the later, softer dampers introduced for cars after February 1985 last rather better. They were fitted post-chassis number 5683149. Despite denials from one source, it appears that you can — and probably should — fit the later dampers to earlier cars, giving an improved ride without any significant penalty in handling. A check on dampers for leakage is a service recommendation at 24,000-mile intervals.

Wheels are alloy, of course, and of different style for the 1.9 from the 1.6. Difficulty may be experienced in finding a tyre-fitting depot which has the correct type of balance weights to fit the wide flange, and probably adhesive ones will have to be used instead.

Inside the car, the most important point to note — saving a search through the handbook — is the location of the fuse box: it drops down from the top of the glove box on the passenger's side, and the relays are behind it. Little problem is experienced with the electric windows and central locking. If there is need for access to the inside of a door, the handles just pull off, armrests are removed after taking out two retaining screws, and trim prises off.

Dim/dip operation of lamps was introduced for 1987, and on these cars the rear fog lamp is usable on main as well as dipped beams; on previous models, it operated only on dipped.

Sealing of the sunroof is by a tube which collapses under vacuum when the operating handle is released. It is as well to allow a second or two for the tube to flatten, releasing the grip on the glass.

Buyers looking for a good used GTI should proceed a little warily, and be guided by a good service history, confirming reasonable mileage. Listen carefully under the bonnet for injector 'rattle', check that the oil pressure is in the middle of the gauge in normal running with the oil fully warmed through, and be alert for any noises warning of excessive wear in the machinery.

In general, the 205GTI is proving to give very good service and to stand up well to the pretty hard driving and high revs which it so invites. Sales of the 1.9 are releasing many 1.6s for the secondhand market, and there are plenty of opportunities to find a really well-preserved example that will give all of the pleasure and liveliness for which the model has become so respected. So if you're in doubt about buying one which does not seem quite what it should be, move on and look elsewhere. It is such a good car that it would be a pity to be landed with a neglected one.

Club activities — GTI line-up on a visit to Paris (left) and members enjoying themselves in the comfort of a hospitality suite at Brands Hatch (right).

JOINING UP

Even if you are not a 'clubby' kind of person, membership of the Peugeot 205GTI Club could be well worth the £10 a year annual subscription.

Established in 1985 with the official backing of Peugeot Talbot, the Club provides a contact point and information for GTI owners through a regular colour magazine, and national and local group meetings. Members qualify for discounts from a number of suppliers on a wide range of accessories, including several featured in this book, and can also purchase GTI leisure wear and other merchandise from the Club.

Some 1,200 205GTI owners are members and the Club has had good support for events as varied as a track day at Ingliston and a trip to Peugeot Talbot Sport in Paris. Motor sport fans are particularly well catered for, since the Club has the use of a hospitality suite for some meetings at Brands Hatch and has arranged special facilities for members at events such as the Lombard RAC Rally and the British Grand Prix.

In May 1986, the first 205GTI National Convention was held at Bruntingthorpe; 750 people enjoyed a host of activities linked to the car and Peugeot's competition involvement.

Paul Kitson, who runs the Club, says that inspiration for it came when they saw that early 205GTI owners were acknowledging each other on the road, as the drivers of traditional British sports cars did in the 1950s and 1960s. Like the Peugeot lion of their advertisements, the Club is going from strength to strength. Contact Paul at: Peugeot 205GTI Club, PO Box 29, Leamington Spa, Warwickshire CV32 5ER. Tel: 0926 316621.

PEUGEOT 205 GTI CLUB
P.O. BOX 29
LEAMINGTON SPA
WARWICKSHIRE
CV32 5ER

For further information please contact
Peugeot 205 GTI Club on telephone: 0926 316621

Added enjoyment

A review of accessories for the 205GTI and the increasing number of special body parts to give it an individual look

Not many options appear in the Peugeot 205GTI catalogue. As befits the top model of the range, several items that might be extras are included in the purchase price: those elegant alloy wheels, supplementary driving lamps, remote-control door mirrors, even the radio/cassette player. Central locking and electric windows are standard on the 1.9 and a combined extra-cost option for the 1.6 GTI and CTI.

In the beginning, the GTI was not quite so well-equipped. Early cars had only a driver's side mirror and the radio was an extra. The factory sunroof, which was not available initially, has always been an option — at £194 in January 1987.

So the choice when ordering a new car is not a very demanding one. Central locking is a nice luxury, even in a small car such as this. Electric windows can be a mixed blessing — they are particularly tiresome if they go wrong, but the Peugeot ones don't have a bad record.

We have to be more hesitant in recommending the Peugeot sunroof, despite its good looks and reasonable price. This well-styled sliding glass panel is mounted on top of rather than within the roof. It can create whistling and booming when closed and an uncomfortable buffetting when open, even at quite modest speeds. 1987 models supplied with a sunroof have a modified windscreen surround which forms a deflector to cure this problem. For earlier cars, an accessory deflector ahead of the sunroof aperture will do the trick — but is not a pretty sight. Some of the after-market sunroof suppliers claim that their roofs do not suffer turbulence problems on the GTI.

Some useful items appear in the official Peugeot Talbot accessory catalogue. The GTI's bright red carpets get dirty quickly so floor mats are really a must. There are several kinds available, though the cheaper ones have a tendency to curl at the corners and get out of shape. Better to choose either the solid rubber type or the special GTI carpet version with the red stripe motif surrounding the plastic heel inserts. For those who want to keep the seats like new, or make some old and 'pulled' seats look better, two types of tailored black-and-red covers are offered, called Monaco and Le Mans.

You don't want to let the occasional bulky load deny you the pleasure of driving a hot hatchback, so a roof rack might be required. Because the 205 does not have conventional rain channels, the regular kind of rack cannot be fitted. Peugeot Talbot have a special one and it does its load-carrying job well enough — though, be warned, it can set up an annoying aerodynamic noise when running 'empty'.

GTI enthusiast Warwick Temple has tested a wide range of accessories for the 205GTI Owners' Club. He reports favourably on a kit providing electric windows, central locking and alarm — all remote-controlled — from Electric Life, of Basingstoke. Fischer, the people who make those C-box cassette holders, offer a special version for the GTI that slots into the bin beneath the radio.

Wheel improvements — pre-1987 GTIs have a coarse plastic rim. There are any number of leather-rimmed alternatives available. Here we show three particularly suitable ones, from the budget-priced Mountney (top) to the leather-bossed Italvolanti Corsa (centre) and the expensive Personal Winner 36 model (bottom).

Still on the inside, changing the steering wheel is the first modification that many owners consider. It is a pity that when the standard wheel looks so good, its thick rim has a coarse-grained plastic cover which can be hard on the hands on a long journey. Peugeot recognized that this was an unpopular piece of price-paring and with the 1987 models fitted a real leather rim. It is, of course, possible to fit the new wheel to an older car, but there are lots of other leather-rimmed wheels available, including the outrageously expensive one from the 205 Turbo 16. Which to choose is a matter of taste and pocket, but a semi-dished 14in wheel gives the same driving position as the standard car. Remember that fitting a smaller-diameter wheel not only may obscure the instruments, but will also make the steering heavier — and it is already quite a weighty proposition for parking.

Most people find the standard seats good enough — even if the specially-designed material wears quickly — but those who feel the need for more support may think the considerable price of a pair of Recaros worthwhile. The GTI's interior trim is not exactly luxurious, with lots of painted metal exposed on the doors, and there are specialists like Cartel, Connolly and Tickford who will happily retrim the whole car in fine leather. But, be warned — that is also a very expensive business.

So much for the inside. What about gilding the lily, giving the outside of your GTI a note of distinction, so that it stands out from the in-crowd? The model is still young, so new items for it are appearing all the time, but it is already

Fischer make a special version of the C-Box cassette holder to fit in the centre console bin of the 205GTI. Neat — but what do you do with the cassette boxes?

Light variations — the Taifun 4 headlamp conversion (top) from Hella provides ABS housings that carry four round 135mm Hella lamp units. Their deeper front spoiler (centre) includes a pair of powerful Optilux driving lights. For maximum illumination and the full rally car look, follow the professionals with separate supplementary lights (bottom).

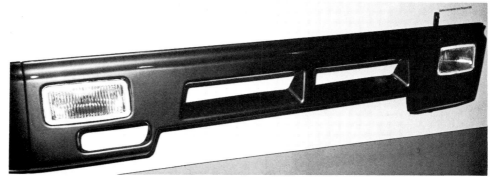

possible to spend £1,500 or more on external body modifications — or add some individual touches for just a few pounds.

Self-adhesive vinyl tape kits provide a low-cost opportunity for appearance changes without repainting. There is a Peugeot Talbot Sport decal set with the red, blue and yellow insignia of the factory rally cars — especially suitable for white GTIs. Other 'graphics kits' provide material with a fine-dot 'screen' that can be used to produce pleasing subtle effects. The trick with this is not to over-do it; a fine stripe or narrow panel is invariably more effective than plastering over most of the body sides. Remember too that these materials are very thin, flexible and many are at least partially transparent, so this is not any easy way of covering scratches and dents...

Reflective rear panels, continuing the line of the rear light across the car and proclaiming the model name, have become fashionable for hot hatchbacks of all kinds. The 205GTI has the advantage over some of its rivals in that the rear number-plate is already beneath the bumper and does not need repositioning, so it is a question of whether you prefer the looks and the extra visibility of a reflective panel to the standard grey corrugated cladding that carries the badges. Peugeot offer a reflective panel carrying the model name big and bold, as do a number of other accessory companies.

Changing the 'face' of the car is an effective way of achieving individuality, and alternative grille and front bumper/spoiler arrangements are becoming available, some incorporating additional lamps. There is a Peugeot-approved four-headlamp grille available in France. A point to be careful of here is that some of these items were designed for the 205 range as a whole and the under-bonnet area is rather more crowded in the GTI than in lesser versions; in at least one type the back of the lamp units foul the fan housing within.

More elaborate panels and complete body kits cover the spectrum from

Securon offer this kit to provide the 205GTI with headlamp wash/wipe. It is wired into the windscreen washer so that the screen and lamps are cleaned simultaneously.

The Peugeot Talbot Sport decal kit provides panels of blue, red and yellow as used by the works rally cars. It looks best on a white car.

A rear reflector panel carrying the model name is available from a number of sources and is easily fixed.

The starting point for body conversion or colour coding — a 205GTI with bumpers and side cladding removed. The bumpers each have four bolts to detach, side cladding is held on by spring clips revealed after sliding off the red stripe trim and the wheelarch extensions are pegged into the wing studs.

Changing the face — the KAT body kit (left) has a new grille and four-lamp front spoiler, while the Cartel front (below) uses a more flared bumper/apron. Zender, Versatec and others offer different front spoiler designs.

elegance to bad taste. Not surprisingly, most attempt to reproduce the appearance of the successful 205 Turbo 16 rally car.

And whatever the makers may pretend, the prime function of these additional body items is appearance. They are most unlikely to show the slightest improvement in the performance, stability or roadholding of a

(Left) More drastic modification can include a new bonnet as well — this one with an air scoop is for the Gutmann turbo engine. (Right) Stand 21 body modifications include this complicated rear wing mounted across the rear window. The lower attachments by self-tapping screws are not very neat. Rear visibility is not seriously affected by this wing, and the wiper operates behind it.

Sill extensions give the car a lower look — these are from Stand 21. An adaptor is supplied to enable the use of the original jack.

standard 205GTI. Peugeot provide it with what their engineers have proved is the optimum combination of aerodynamic features for everyday road use.

While one should take claims of aerodynamic advantages and wind-tunnel 'optimization' with a pinch of salt, it is advisable to go for components that have at least been properly tested. It is all too easy to ruin the aerodynamics of the original car by sticking too large a spoiler in the wrong place.

Warwick Temple's car shows the complete Stand 21 kit, made in France and supplied in Britain by David Sears Motorsport. It consists of four sets of components, made in ABS, and this reasonably priced kit is intended to be relatively simple for an owner to fit — though he has to plan painting carefully if he wants the result to be fully colour-coded.

The full Dimma T16 body kit, supplied through AIP Mouldings, and fitted to the Skip Brown Lynx, is intended to give a Turbo 16 look. It is a complicated (and expensive) 10-part kit, some of the glass-fibre parts requiring bonding to the metal. Like other kits with extended wheelarches, it needs wide wheels to complete the visual effect.

There are a number of suppliers of 205GTI body kits that are confined to front and rear aprons and side skirts. This one is in glass-fibre from Cartel Cars and Conversions.

There was a time when this kind of body reshaping would have been a job for a specialist coachbuilder, working in aluminium, hand-beaten and riveted into place. Today's body kits are invariably additional cladding, prefabricated in plastic, and requiring no cutting of material from the original body. Most offered for the 205GTI so far are glass-fibre, which is a perfectly satisfactory material for car bodies, as Lotus and others will testify, and relatively inexpensive. But some other plastics, like ABS and polyurethane, that can be more accurately — and expensively — moulded, are also used. ABS can look good, but is prone to crack after a light knock and can't be repaired satisfactorily; for less vulnerable items, like grille panels, it is ideal. The advantage of flexible polyurethane, formed by the RIM (Reaction Injection Moulding) process, is that it can cope with light impacts by deforming and returning to its original shape. The 205GTI's rear lip spoiler is formed from semi-rigid polyurethane foam, which has the consistency and appearance of hard rubber.

Since the kits come with fitting instructions, it is tempting to regard their application as a do-it-yourself job. And so it can be for the skilled and patient with some experience of bodywork. Some of the kits can be supplied with the new parts ready-sprayed in standard Peugeot colours, which can ease one of the major problems. But for most of us, the more comprehensive kits require professional attention.

The professionals pre-fit the components, fettling them for their precise location (even if the parts themselves are precision-made it is surprising how much apparently identical bodyshells vary from one to another). They are then painted off the car before being fitted — usually with bolts, clip fasteners, self-tapping screws or pop-rivets, but sometimes also by bonding (the latter with a 'two pack' adhesive).

Glass-fibre components are usually supplied in primer, while ABS parts are invariably black. If you have a black car, or are prepared for a colour contrast, the ABS can be polished. Painting can be tricky as not only does an exact match have to be made with the body colour, but the characteristics of the material must also be considered. The same paint may look different on plastic alongside steel. Some plastics are very solvent-sensitive, while others, designed to be flexible in use, need a higher proportion of plasticizers in the paint than the rigid ones.

Painting all the exterior trim, including the bumpers and side-cladding, in body colour is an increasingly popular technique, though much more successful with some colours than others. Wheels can also be colour-coded to enhance the all-over effect.

Since the GTI's wheels intentionally resemble those of the Turbo 16, if the idea of customizing is to produce a front-wheel-drive Group B replica there will not be much point in changing them. The standard alloy wheels are a quality product, by Speedline in Italy. The choice of alternatives is enormous. Take care

A rather different approach from Aston Martin designer William Towns — his P'Zazz is a set of self-coloured glass-fibre panels that fit over existing lower panels and bumpers.

Prototype of an Italian body kit from Bubble Car, handled in Britain by Dream Wheelers, of Bedford.

Kurt Gutmann, in Germany, is one of the best-known Peugeot tuners and his products are imported to Britain by GM Design, of Bristol. This is their original Turbolook body kit, made in glass-fibre with Kevlar reinforcement. It is recommended for professional installation.

Crown UK of Newcastle upon Tyne make a 205GTI body kit in glass-fibre — there is a picture of it being fitted on page 66 — and it has been adopted by Peugeot Talbot Birmingham main dealer George Heath Motors for this special edition based on the 1.9 GTI.

Gutmann's Racing Look kit, introduced for 1987, can be applied to the 205CTI Cabriolet.

to ensure that the inset and wheel nut location and type are right; wheels designed for Fords will fit, up to 7in rim width and in 13, 14 or 15in diameter.

The bigger the diameter of the wheel, the lower the profile of tyre will be needed (50-series with 15in) but any wider section than 195 can present clearance problems. 205-section tyres can be fitted to the standard rims with 4mm clearance spacers at the rear but they can foul the front of the rear wheelarches when the car is loaded.

Changing wheels can be an expensive business. Quality is important — and tends to be proportional to price. (There is reassurance in one of the four international safety standards — BS AU50 Part 2, TUV (Germany), JWL (Japan) and SEMA 5.1A (USA).) You can pay as little as £30 or as much as £200 per wheel. Then there is the cost of four (possibly five) new tyres to consider. It is not hard to spend £1,000 on a set of new 'boots' — and since the discarded ones won't be worth much unless they are brand new it is probably a good idea to plan the switch when the original tyres are wearing out.

Bearing in mind this investment, you might like to select a wheel pattern that incorporates a lockable hub cap, or fit locking hub nuts. Perhaps security measures like etching the car's registration number on its windows, and fitting an alarm system, should have preceded the more pleasurable accessories and modifications described in this chapter. It is a sad fact that the more attractive you make your car, the more it will receive not only admiring glances, but also undesirable attention. So take precautions!

Getting converted

Ways of making the quick GTI faster still, and other mechanical modifications, investigated by Jeremy Walton

JEREMY WALTON probably has more experience of tuned and modified cars than any writer in Britain. They have been a special interest for him since his early journalistic work at *Cars & Car Conversions* and *Motoring News* in the 1960s and early 1970s. He writes for those two magazines today, as well as *Performance Car* and many others.

Tuned GTI shoot-out — Autocar ran a back-to-back test of the Skip Brown GTiS and the Cheetah from Charters of Aldershot in April 1986. Both offered 1.9-litre engines before the factory model, the Skip Brown Cars version having a bigger-valve head. Though the two cars are of rather different character, the magazine thought honours were divided.

The 205GTI is fast becoming the most popular of subjects among the conversion specialists. Even the latest and very rapid 1.9-litre version is finding favour as the basis for further development.

As you will know by now, the standard GTI comes at three levels of power — the 1.6-litre with 105bhp, uprated to 115bhp from mid-1986, and the 130bhp 1.9. It sounds like a good idea to use factory parts to bring the earlier 1.6 engines up to the output of the latest version, but for what is involved — bigger valves,

Turbocharging specialists Janspeed elected to use a mechanical supercharger for their 205GTI conversion, shown in prototype form at the 1986 British Motor Show. Skip Brown also offer a supercharged model, using a Sprintex blower.

different camshaft, etc — the cost scarcely justifies the improvement. If you are going to spend serious money on the 105bhp engine, it is worth being rather more ambitious.

The Peugeot factory announced a 125bhp engine kit at the time of the GTI's introduction and it remains in the official Peugeot Talbot Sport catalogue as Fast Road Kit, part number 7000. With a 1987 price of £985, ex-VAT and without fitting, it isn't cheap (though a £150 exchange allowance is made for the standard cylinder head, provided it is in good condition).

The kit consists of a cylinder head with modified combustion chambers, 41.5mm inlet and 34.5mm exhaust valves, and a high-lift camshaft. The compression ratio is raised marginally from 10.2:1 to 10.3:1. Its rating is actually 123.3bhp at 6,700rpm, 700rpm beyond the standard engine's peak. The torque increase is more modest — 105lb/ft at 4,200 rather than 4,000rpm.

In 1985 I tested a GTI with such a kit installed for *Performance Car*. We measured its performance electronically on two occasions. The first time round it was only fractionally quicker than Peugeot Talbot's standard-specification demonstrator. We discovered that the rev-limiter had not been re-set; a Tachymetric relay is now included in the kit for earlier cars (prior to chassis number 55366101). The second test, with 7,000rpm available and utilized in

Though author Walton shares most British tuners' scepticism about turbo conversions for the GTI, long-time German tuner Kurt Gutmann has offered them successfully for some time. His 1.6-litre turbo develops 148bhp, while the 1.9 is up to 175bhp.

A Gutmann 1.9 turbo with Turbolook 2 body kit. During German TÜV certification tests a car of this specification recorded 139mph!

seductively smooth bursts, was much more rewarding. The 0-60mph acceleration dropped a few hundredths below 8sec and more than 7sec was cut from the 0-100mph time. Top speed was up from the standard car's 115.4mph to 123.3mph. Average fuel consumption — excluding the 17.9mpg performance-testing session — increased from 29.4 to 28.4mpg.

In an otherwise fairly standard GTI (apart from lots of body stripes that brought comments like 'who was that bumblebee I saw you with last night?'), there were some penalties to be paid for the extra urge. The chief disadvantage of the Fast Road Kit — and the production 115bhp engine in my experience — is that flexibility in high gears suffers and the tickover becomes a tiny off-beat anthem, testifying to the rebellious new camshaft. Unlike the old days of tuned Minis and the like, this idling roughness does not bring a tendency to stall; the fuel injection system maintains the modified car's 1,100rpm tickover. But it leaves one in no doubt that this is hot stuff, approaching 80bhp per litre...

The Fast Road Kit is not intended for competition and the 205GTI will not comply with Group N or Group A regulations thus modified. If you want to compete under these rules, the Peugeot Talbot Sport Special Tuning Kits & Parts list includes a range of approved components for engine, transmission and chassis.

The list is available from Peugeot Talbot Sport's customer department at Humber Road, Coventry. This 'department within a department', managed by Tim Millington, works alongside Des O'Dell's competition team. Their wares are available from selected Peugeot Talbot dealers.

An alternative roadgoing conversion for the 105bhp 1.6 is available from Skip Brown Cars, of Ridley Green, near Tarporley in Cheshire. This Road Speed kit gives an extra 21bhp using an uprated cylinder head, high-lift camshaft and stainless-steel valves of similar dimensions to the non-stainless ones used by the factory for the 115bhp model. Detail work on the head comprises equalizing the combustion chamber volumes and polishing but not significantly enlarging the inlet and exhaust ports. The price of £625 (ex-VAT) covers a workshop fitting service, exchanging standard components for the modified kit.

Skip Brown, a company with an honourable record with the products of Peugeot Talbot and its predecessors in Coventry, including the Sunbeam-Lotus and Ti and rally Avengers, now specialize in 205GTI conversions. Like the Cheetah, developed by Paul Burch and available from Peugeot Talbot dealers Charters of Aldershot, they beat the factory in offering a 1.9-litre GTI.

Skip Brown have a straightforward conversion providing new crankshaft, connecting rods and lead-bronze bearings but using the original 1.6 head and camshaft, which costs £995 and offers up to 30% more power. A more elaborate kit, RS2015, also includes a gas-flowed cylinder head and enlarged valves. This 1,905cc motor, with which Skip Brown fit an oil cooler, costs £1,380

GTI's big sister

A world class rally car that resembled the production GTI was a key part of Peugeot's stategy. Martin Sharp traces the development of the 205 Turbo 16

This is what is meant by a 'homologation special' — the 200 Turbo 16s required to qualify for Group B lined up for FISA inspection.

MARTIN SHARP is deputy editor of *Cars & Car Conversions*, having previously worked at Ford's Advanced Vehicle Operation. He has made a special study of the rally supercars that were produced under the Group B regulations and has experience of road and rally versions of the 205 Turbo 16. Martin was highly commended for his technical writing in the 1986 Periodical Publishers Association awards.

At the end of rallying's 'two-wheel-drive' era, the Peugeot Group had some useful success. A Sunbeam-Lotus won the 1980 Lombard RAC Rally and the 1981 World Rally Championship, but this was badged a Talbot. The creation of Talbot as a separate marque, following Peugeot's acquisition of Chrysler Europe, had served to confuse rather than aid the Group's marketing programme. Eventually it was decided to combine the Peugeot and Talbot brands and emphasize the Group name. Motor sport was identified as important in creating a new image for Peugeot and its forthcoming small car — the M24, that was to become the 205.

The option was there to continue Talbot's Formula 1 involvement with Ligier and Matra, but this three-way relationship was not the easiest and in the eyes of the public was eclipsed by Renault's independent Grand Prix effort. Automobiles Peugeot president Jean Boillot concluded that world-class rallying with a Peugeot product provided the best chance of achieving their objectives. Thus, the 'M24-Rally' project came into being.

Peugeot had made a name for themselves in African rallying using modified

The shape and dimensions are close to the 205GTI, but the Turbo 16 could not be more different under the skin — offset mid-mounted engine, four-wheel-drive and competition-car adjustable suspension characterize this strictly two-seater 205.

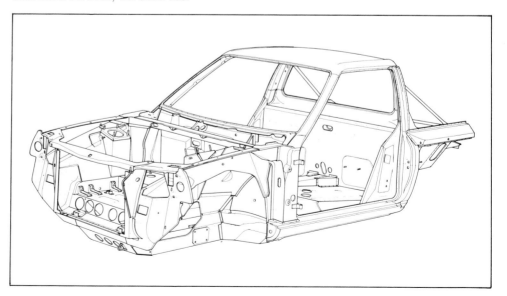

The 205 Turbo 16's hull has a stout monocoque centre section and front end, but the engine and the rear of the transmission are supported on sub-frames and all body panels are made in plastics.

mainstream production cars — they won the Safari six times between 1963 and 1978 — and in later years an ambitious co-driver named Jean Todt had played an increasingly important role in their team organization for these tough events.

But international rallying was changing. Audi had shown that four-wheel-drive could be devastatingly effective. Turbocharging had brought rally car power outputs to a new high. Todt outlined ideas for an even more radical new generation of rally competitor to Boillot. In October 1981, the Peugeot cars chief put Jean Todt in charge of Peugeot Talbot Sport and the M24-Rally began to take shape.

That shape, significantly, bore a direct relationship to the mainstream M24. It was clear from the outset that, mechanically, the rally car would have to be unique, but if it was to be truly effective in promoting the image of the everyday models it needed to *look* as much like them as possible.

Peugeot exterior styling boss, Gerard Welter, is a motor sport enthusiast of the most committed kind — he is the 'W' of the Peugeot-powered WM Le Mans cars — and he relished the idea of a 'silhouette' rally car. He sketched ideas for the production version of the M24-Rally, for under the new Group B regulations, 200 of any such vehicle would have to be made.

At the La Garenne research centre in the Paris suburbs, a M24-Rally project team was established. Bernard Perron was appointed 'architect', Hubert Allera was put in charge of the design team responsible for mechanical components, and Todt brought in experienced rally engineer Jean-Claude Vaucard. Peugeot Talbot Sport's UK competitions manager Des O'Dell — who had been responsible for the Sunbeam-Lotus programme — moved to Paris to take charge of prototype build, though he was later to return to his job in Coventry.

Though the concept of a mid-engined car with four-wheel drive was agreed early on, how its power should be produced was a major topic of discussion within the design team. The rally-experienced engineers advocated a large-capacity, normally-aspirated engine, but the powers-that-be in the company saw advantages in a smaller, supercharged power unit, closer to 205 production configuration. They prevailed. A turbocharged 16-valve four-cylinder engine was to be used, which gave rise to the M24-Rally's official name: 205 Turbo 16.

The basic design was finalized in July 1982. As development gathered pace it became apparent that an 'evolution' of the car would be allowed under the Group B rules — that is, that certain improvements could be made to the homologated car without the need to produce another 200. Evolution modifications need be incorporated in just 10% of the original production quantity — 20 cars.

Jean-Claude Vaucard recalls that this complicated the project considerably: 'If we had known that evolution would be allowed when we started, we wouldn't have made the car exactly as we did. The decision obliged us to

Opening the bonnet of
the Turbo 16 means
lifting the whole of the
rear bodywork to reveal
the engine to the right-
hand side, looking quite
small and insignificant
compared with the
trunking to the
turbocharger intercooler
and heat-shielding of
the exhaust.

Heart of a mid-1980s
rally supercar is its four-
wheel-drive
transmission. This
diagram shows all the
elements of the
Peugeot's drive-line,
from its four-valves-per-
cylinder twin-cam turbo
engine to the transverse
five-speed gearbox and
transfer gear, via a
viscous coupling to a
conventional limited-slip
rear differential and
prop-shaft to a 'free'
differential at the front.

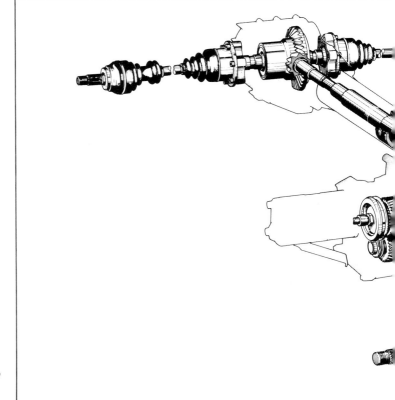

change a lot of parts, which increased the cost a great deal.'

The advent of the evolution Group B car meant that the 205 Turbo 16 would have to be produced in two versions: an out-and-out rally car taking full advantage of the regulations and an exotic road car. However, Bernard Perron explains that the need to sell the latter was always secondary: 'We thought "rally car" all the time during the development — no compromise.'

Vaucard and test driver Jean-Pierre Nicolas set about devising the first evolution 205 Turbo 16, the E1. The basis with which they had to work was sound but sophisticated: a monocoque-style chassis containing a mid-located, 1,775cc 16-valve, turbocharged four-cylinder engine driving all four wheels. The engine was based around the alloy XU cylinder block fitted to the standard 205GTI and other PSA road car derivatives, but its combination of twin-camshaft cylinder head, intercooled turbocharger, K-Jetronic fuel injection and transistorized ignition was unique to the T16's specification. In 200-off homologation specification the unit produced 200bhp, but even in first evolution guise the rally engine was capable of at least 320bhp.

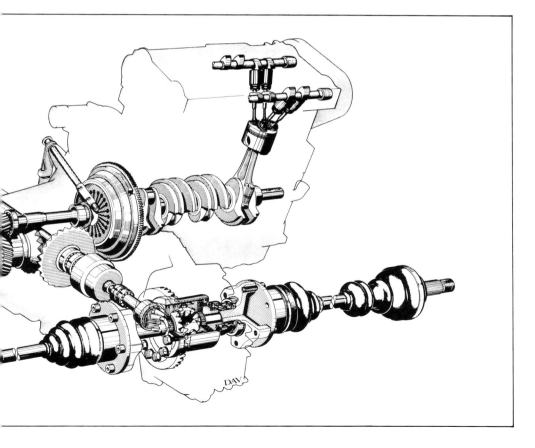

Stark and purposeful — 205 Turbo 16's cockpit is designed to do a job, rather than look pretty. Heater/ventilator control console is one of the few carry-overs from regular 205s, while the steering wheel is different but has GTI style.

Also unique to the T16 was — and still is — the way its power train is arranged. The engine and its Citroën SM-derived synchromesh gearbox sit transversely in the car, just behind the occupants, with the engine biased to the right-hand side. All T16s are left-hand drive, so this makes the car about 50kg heavier on the co-driver's side, and while cynics initially suggested that this was in order to counterbalance the substantial weight of Jean-Pierre 'Jumbo' Nicolas, attention to the amount of fuel carried in each of the separate tanks under the occupants' seats — maintaining 55 litres in the left-hand tank at all times — brings the T16's right-hand weight bias to an average of about 20kg.

Apart from enabling the designers to maintain the compact exterior dimensions required, an advantage in this layout is the release of precious space for ancillaries above the gearbox. It also allows comparatively easy access to the belts and equipment on the engine's front face in the car's right-hand flank, and to the torque-splitting equipment on the end of the gearbox at the other side.

By 1982, Audi had convincingly demonstrated the advantages of four-wheel drive. The 205 Turbo 16's transmission system represented a second generation of four-wheel drive technology. Its easily-accessed torque-splitting equipment consists of an epicyclic train differential, which operates in conjunction with a fluid-filled viscous coupling to direct torque to each axle in ratios which correspond to the epicyclic gearing. The front/rear options range from 48/52 to 25/75, and early tests with the E1 showed 34/66 to be optimum for gravel rallying and 25/75 for tarmac, while a 45/55 torque ratio — exactly the same as the early car's static front/rear weight distribution — was found ideal where weight transfer is at a minimum under snow-ridden, minimum-traction conditions.

Siting a viscous coupling in this so-called centre differential enables torque to be provided to the axle with the most available traction. The road-going T16 and the first rally developments had a mechanical limited-slip differential in the rear axle only. In later rally car development, as power increased, PTS provided mechanical slip limiting in each axle so that the torque could be made to go where it would be of most use — to the wheel(s) with most available traction.

Devising the optimum suspension for this new configuration of car took much of the design team's attention. The T16 was homologated with single dampers at each wheel. It originally ran with Peugeot-branded all-hydraulic units, but PTS soon called in Bilstein. Yet even with the German gas-filled units installed, the team worked long and hard to optimize damping performance and reliability. PTS now admit that ideally the car should have been homologated with twin dampers per wheel at the rear.

During the development of the E1 car in late 1983, PTS took on a major asset in the person of Jean-Pierre Boudy. He had been a leading light in turbocharged engine development at Renault Sport, and brought his now-famous 'DPV' system with him to Peugeot-Talbot Sport. This cleverly-considered aspiration equipment was responsible for Bernard Perron's early comment: 'We don't know what turbo lag is'. DPV stands for *Dispositif Pre-rotation Variable* (Variable Pre-rotation Device) and provides varied air quantities at optimum angles to the compressor wheel of the turbocharger *in advance* of the rotation period during which the compressor turbine will require those conditions. It was a refinement which contributed a great deal to the driveability of the T16.

Shortly after Boudy's arrival, André de Cortanze joined the team as chief of the technical department. He joined on January 1, 1984 and worked with Vaucard toward the car's competition debut in Corsica that year.

When the car was announced, in February 1983, Peugeot's stated objective was: 'To make the 205 Turbo 16 the last word in rally cars'. A year later the resolve remained; 1984 was to be a testing year, and PTS said that it intended the 205 Turbo 16 to win the 1985 World Rally Championship. It did.

The 200-off road car and 20 E1 versions were homologated into Group B in April 1984. In its 'testing year' the T16 achieved its first World Rally Championship event win at the Rally of the 1000 Lakes, in Finland, and then went on to win the final two events in the series, the Sanremo and RAC Rallies.

At a stroke, Peugeot had rewritten the rally car rule book, and in so doing had also changed the parameters for 'homologation specials'. While Ford Escorts and Fiat Abarths had been built in modified forms and in the correct quantities to suit a competition purpose, the first truly purpose-built homologation special was the Lancia Stratos. The 205 Turbo 16 was the first true purpose-built four-wheel drive homologation special.

The road-going T16, however, is similar only in concept to the works rally cars; many of the important details are quite different. In keeping with Bernard Perron's original philosophy, this 200bhp road car exhibits many rally car traits in its character — while driving in traffic, occupants can hear its coil springs and 17-panel bodywork exercising themselves; storage space is at a premium; and high-speed long-distance travel precludes the use of a radio. For the occupants of a road-going T16 there is no question about the machine's heritage.

The road-going 205 Turbo 16's chassis and transmission give it remarkably stable characteristics both in 'attack mode' on rural routes, and while rushing kilometres under its wheels along *autobahnen*. Under almost all road-driving conditions, the 200-off T16's chassis performance is sure, secure, stimulating, undiluted driving fun.

Going really quickly in the road car, however, can be something of a struggle at times. The car's forced-induction apparatus only operates properly above 3,700rpm, and turbo lag can be measured in seconds. This means learning a new driving style involving unnatural throttle applications, judicious use of the gearbox, and constant attention to keeping the turbocharger spinning.

PTS were aware that some 16 customers would want to rally their cars, and that the £25,000 road-going version would be well off the pace. Accordingly, in early 1986, a series of kits were made available to convert the road-going car into a 'clubman' rally machine. At a total cost nearly $1\frac{1}{2}$ times that of the original *complete* car, the four resulting kits were not cheap, but they transformed the road car into a 300bhp machine which was effectively just below E1 rally specification.

A year to the month after the 205 Turbo 16 was first homologated, the works team introduced a second evolution version. Work had started on E2 in July 1984 and it was homologated in time to compete in the 1985 Tour de Corse.

Jean-Pierre Boudy ensured that a minimum of 435bhp and a much wider torque band would be available by revising the inlet ports in the cylinder head, fitting a near-Formula 1-size Garrett turbocharger in place of the previous KKK unit, engineering sensor-adjusted electronic rather than mechanical control of the DPV, and adding a water injection system.

The essential chassis tasks were to make the whole machine stronger in torsion and lighter overall. The central monocoque section was not changed, but cooling media were moved to the front, where detail lightening was achieved, and major changes were made to the rear. Here, the previous monocoque extension arms and heavy crossmember were replaced by a tubular structure. The result was a 30% more rigid structure in torsion, a total of 20kg of lost weight, and an improved front/rear weight distribution of very close to 50/50.

Timo Salonen had complained of heavy steering in the E1 car, so Vaucard engineered power steering into the E2 version for him — an even more important modification with so much more torque going through the front wheels. Also homologated for the E2 car was a water-cooling system for the shock absorbers. A sensor at the bottom of the right-hand rear shock absorber, which always ran hottest because it carried most load, monitored damper temperature. On events such as the Safari Rally, when these temperatures became critical, water could be sprayed through injectors on to the outer body

The £25,000 'standard' 205 Turbo 16 is a nervous thoroughbred, lots of fun to drive, though not outstandingly fast against the stopwatch, as the performance figures show. Contrast the original 'homologation' car with its final, Evolution 2 development, which first appeared in mid-1985. Undeniably, some of the visual links with the GTI were lost in the interests of improved aerodynamics.

of the shock absorbers to cool them. This could be achieved either automatically, or by the co-driver kicking a pedal when the damper temperature read-out on the dashboard told him to do so.

The 205 Turbo 16 has exhibited one worrying characteristic from birth. Rally cars, being subject to excessively bumpy roads, are not always on the ground, and on events like the Rally of the 1000 Lakes, in Finland, tend to spend quite a lot of time aviating. In early tests, it was discovered that the T16 didn't jump very well, and the important part of the process was the way it landed.

PTS first worked with Aerospatiale in an attempt to adjust the aerodynamics of the car and minimize this problem. While an improvement of 10-20% was achieved, it was felt that attention to the car's suspension would reap bigger rewards. A 3-metre jump was built at an off-road driving school near Paris, where it was soon discovered that the suspension was not the major contributor to the problem.

The difficulty was that, once the T16 becomes airborne, if its engine speed was then increased, its nose was forced upwards violently — enough to shock men of the calibre of Ari Vatanen sufficiently to make him lift off the throttle. As soon as the engine speed dropped, the opposite occured; the T16's flight plan aborted itself, the car pivoted around its mid-point, and the nose dropped alarmingly towards the ground.

Vaucard explains: 'It is impossible for the drivers to react instinctively to the car's changes in attitude when it flies. Sometimes they arrive too fast at a jump and are obliged to brake. It's a very rare case when all the conditions are perfect; when they brake hard just as the car starts to climb and then accelerate when they are at the top of the climb'.

Unique to the Peugeot as a four-wheel-drive rally car is its transversely-positioned power train. Not only are all wheels rotating in the same direction and linked to the driver's right foot, the crankshaft rotation direction means that the major engine rotating parts are in exactly the same situation — spinning the same way and linked to the throttle. The combined inertia of all these rotating masses under rapid rates of rpm change seems certain to be the prime cause of the Turbo 16's fear of flying. A French student spent his vacation programming a study into the inertial effects on a free-flight 205 T16 of various rates of change in its rotating masses. He went back to university, program unfinished.

The Turbo 16's birthday in April 1986 was celebrated by homologating a six-speed gearbox, primarily for use on long events such as the Safari Rally. During the year, modifications were also made to reinforce the cylinder block. Wheel diameters went up an inch to 16in, so the suspension geometry needed adjusting accordingly, and bigger brake discs could be accommodated. PTS grabbed this opportunity to install new open-backed brake calipers and redesign the shape of the wheels for tarmac use, casting ventilator fans into the wheel to aid hub, suspension and brake cooling. The gravel wheel design remained virtually closed to avoid dirt ingress.

1986, though, was the year when it was announced that Group B was to die and its planned successor, Group S, was not to be. Before FISA's May decision, Peugeot were working toward a third evolution version of the Turbo 16. In particular, the team was researching ways to improve the efficiency ·of the four-wheel drive system and thereby the car's handling. Although none of these transmission ideas reached the test stage before May 1986, they had looked set to make the Peugeot rally car yet again the first to compete with a new generation of four-wheel drive. Two concepts existed; one using variable-efficiency mechanical limited-slip differentials, the other a particularly innovative multi-viscous coupling and free-wheel system.

The Peugeot 205 Turbo 16 won the Rally of the 1000 Lakes in September and went on to take the 1986 World Championship. The expert on-event assistance of engineer Vaucard, however, was not available to the team after Finland.

Something completely different — the Quasar show car is a further 'image enhancer' for Peugeot, which combines a two-seater sports car body with a 205 Turbo 16 engine and transmission, exposed at the rear like a motorcycle.

He was in France and Africa, testing and developing the lengthened version of the car for the 1987 Paris-Dakar Rally. Stretched to accommodate a massive 290-litre extra fuel load, well over the maximum 110-litre capacity of the rally car, it was a sophisticated machine in its own right, but far removed from the innovative final rally version. 'To develop this car I have had to do the inverse of what I was thinking about for the Group B car. It had to be reliable, more simple to service.'

It was, and Peugeot won Paris-Dakar at their first attempt. But Group B and the World Rally Championship programme are over. Vaucard reflects: 'You really can't understand exactly what happened for Peugeot Talbot Sport — we started from zero three years ago. We were three people at the beginning, with no workshop installations, no people. We said we were going to contest World Championship rallies and we made a car. We had everything to do to start from zero. And then, when everything was going good — *finito!* It just doesn't seem possible'.

Performance

The test team at *Autocar* have subjected three versions of the 205 Turbo 16 to full performance measurement. The figures for the 'standard' roadgoing homologation car make an interesting comparison with the 205GTI performance detailed on page 45. The Evolution 1 version was tested in August 1985, the Evolution 2 after the 1986 Lombard RAC Rally. Both were cars run by Peugeot Talbot Sport UK for Mikael Sundstrom and to full works specification.

	205 Turbo 16	Evolution 1	Evolution 2
0-30mph	2.5 sec	1.6 sec	1.3 sec
0-40mph	3.9	2.2	1.9
0-50mph	5.3	3.2	2.4
0-60mph	7.8	4.3	3.3
0-70mph	10.0	5.2	4.2
0-80mph	12.6	6.3	5.3
0-90mph	16.4	7.9	6.4
0-100mph	21.7	9.4	8.0
0-110mph	29.1	11.6	9.5

Evolution, Peugeot style — how the works 205 Turbo 16 changed, from the more powerful but outwardly 'clean' E1 to the be-winged E2 of even higher performance. These photographs were taken in 1985, on the Acropolis and 1000 Lakes, respectively, both of which were won by team driver Timo Salonen on the way to his and Peugeot's first World Championship.

Double World Champion

Peter Newton follows the short but glorious World Championship history of the 205 Turbo 16 — three years that brought 17 wins and two world titles

Ari Vatanen stood at Calvi, a rustic township perched precariously on the rocky outcrops of the north-west coast of Corsica. Two-thirds of the Tour de Corse had been completed, his lead was an impressive 1min 47sec over the first of the Lancias driven by fellow-Finn Markku Alen.

As the rain drummed wildly on Calvi's racketing window panes that night and a storm-force wind wailed like a banshee through the town's narrow cobble-stoned alleys, Vatanen was on the threshold of a dream. A debut victory was in prospect with an all-new car in a World Championship rally. He had already accumulated seven fastest and five second-fastest times on the 19 preceding special stages. Now, with 431 kilometres of tortuous switchback roads to go and a change in the weather that would ease the car's problem of overheating brakes, Vatanen and the Peugeot 205 Turbo 16 were aiming for a place in motor sporting history.

Vatanen's dream ended when the little car plunged off the road in a maelstrom of Kevlar, glass-fibre and twisted metal. But the 1984 Tour de Corse had shown that, henceforth, rallying would never be quite the same again.

1984 was intended merely as a dress rehearsal for Peugeot's full assault on the World Rally Championship in 1985. The long asphalt special stages in Corsica had shown up a braking problem, which was tackled with typical gusto by technical director André de Cortanze and chief engineer Jean-Claude Vaucard.

Peugeot Talbot Sport director Jean Todt had identified two events that represented the sternest gravel rally challenges — the 1000 Lakes in Finland and the Acropolis Rally in Greece. The latter would be the car's first major rough road test. Todt, a perfectionist and compulsive worrier, was anxious about the new car's ability to cope with the pounding it would receive in Europe's roughest rally.

PETER NEWTON has a long and deep interest in rallying, as a participant and as a reporter. He was rallies editor of *Autosport*, then editor of *Cars & Car Conversions* for eight years, before joining Avenue Communications, a public relations consultancy which has close links with motor sport. He drives a 205GTI.

Peugeot's star performers — Ari Vatanen, (left), scored three wins in a row in 1984 and two more in 1985; (centre), Timo Salonen had five wins on the way to his 1985 World title; and Juha Kankkunen, (right), emerged as 1986 champion after late-season controversy.

With some doubts still surrounding the integrity of the Turbo 16's chassis, the director's worries were not without foundation, but by the end of the Acropolis first leg, Vatanen, recovered from the chipped shoulder blade and serious bruising he had received in Corsica, was just 1 second behind Walter Rohrl's Audi Quattro.

French hopes soared the next day, when Vatanen elbowed past Rohrl into the lead, but the moment of glory was to be short-lived as a broken oil pump belt and then a turbocharger failure eventually led to retirement.

The team's handling of the crisis, in particular the quick and efficient turbocharger change, was as encouraging as Vatanen's gravel road performance. Team-mate Jean-Pierre Nicolas, who had finished fourth in the team's Corsican debut, was unlucky to retire on the last night in Greece when a brake caliper broke and destroyed the car's suspension. Though they didn't finish, Peugeot had a scent of victory.

Two months later, in August, the 1000 Lakes Rally was to see the promise fulfilled. Work had begun on the Evolution 2 model, while modifications to the E1 were made as a result of the Acropolis experience. For Finland, ex-Renault Formula 1 engine man Jean-Pierre Boudy found more punch in the power unit, bringing it up to 350bhp.

Todt's worries in Finland were about the car's reactions to the 1000 Lakes' notorious jumps. The director had experienced these for himself, strapped in alongside Vatanen. The car suffered a series of violent oscillations on touchdown after a typical Finnish 'flight' and it required all of Vatanen's lightning reactions to keep it on the road.

This was 48 hours before the start. On the morning of the event new dampers arrived from Bilstein in Germany — a magnificent response to an 'impossible' last-minute request — but they arrived too late to be fitted before the start. By Todt's perfectionist standards, Peugeot began their third World Championship rally in disarray.

In fact, what emerged in Finland was evidence of the team's ability to fine-tune its cars under pressure. As the rally progressed, de Cortanze and his technicians strove to find the right balance for the chassis.

It also brought out the best in Ari Vatanen, who was cool under pressure — something for which he had not always been noted. He drove with smoothness and maturity, taking the lead by the 14th special stage and thereafter dominating this most competitive of events. After the 1984 1000 Lakes one eminent rally journalist was moved to write: 'In three scant rallies Peugeot have achieved something that some teams will never emulate in a decade'.

Jean Todt remembers the emotion of their first victory: 'I ran to the finishing line of the last stage. Ari drove up to us. De Cortanze and Boudy were crying, while Jacques Delubac and I also had tears in our eyes. Ari and Terry Harryman

Nearly a dream debut — Ari Vatanen dominated the first half of the 1984 Tour de Corse in the 205 Turbo 16's first event.

were not much better. No-one said a word. I phoned Jean Boillot (Peugeot's president) from my car and said, "Sir, we have won!"'

Boillot's decision to enhance Peugeot's image through rallying was already paying off.

Two cars were entered for the Sanremo Rally in the autumn. Competitive with the Lancia 037s on tarmac, the 205 was untouchable on the loose. The Italians could do nothing to stop Vatanen dominating their home event. On his way to victory, he recorded 31 fastest times out of 54 special stages, though there was a scare on the final night when he went off the road briefly during a thunderstorm.

The team then left for Africa, for testing in preparation for the following year's Safari Rally. After consecutive rally wins it was to be a salutary return to earth, for the cars broke and one was burnt-out. There was, however, one last 'rehearsal' before the big push in 1985 — the Lombard RAC Rally of Great Britain.

In recent years, the RAC had become something of an Audi benefit, rather as it had been for Ford in the 1970s. A solitary Peugeot stood between the Germans and another walkover and it proved more than equal to the task. Despite a lapse from Vatanen late in the event, and then a broken drive-shaft that allowed Mikkola's Audi back into the lead, the 205 Turbo 16 was once again able to dominate the rally. The omens for the following year were good.

With three wins in the 1984 World Rally Championship behind them, Peugeot started favourite in the 1985 Monte Carlo Rally, still rallying's most famous event.

For rally enthusiasts, Peugeot's victory in the 1985 Monte was one for the history books. Vatanen had a comfortable lead, but it was instantly wiped out when co-driver Terry Harryman incurred an 8-minute penalty at Gap for booking into the control 4 minutes early. Recovering 8 minutes in the distance left looked impossible, even for the brilliant Finn. What followed is best described by Jean Todt:

'Before leaving Gap, Ari stunned me by saying calmly: "We'll win anyhow". I didn't believe him but nodded my head. For everyone else the matter was closed, the rally was already won by Audi.

'After each stage I talked with Ari and found his resolve firm. He persisted in trying to pace himself so as to have a tiny chance in the last kilometres to fight with everything he had.

'At the St Raphael Pass Ari had to make a crucial tyre choice. He would face 8 kilometres of snow going uphill, and 22 kilometres of dry, wide road going down. Racing tyres guaranteed performance, snow tyres ensured safety. We all offered our opinions, but such a decision is ultimately in the hands of the driver.

'Rohrl drove past, his car fitted with racing tyres. "Snow tyres," Ari said, after some hesitation. I turned to André, saying, "this is where the rally will be won or not". A few minutes later, I called René Issart, who had a direct line to the stage

Former Grand Prix star Carlos Reutemann was brought into the Peugeot works team for the 1985 Rally of Argentina. His progress created tremendous local publicity and the results were good, too — third place overall. This was the event in which Ari Vatanen crashed heavily, putting himself out of rallying for over a year.

finish. "Don't move, we're checking on it now", he said.... "someone's coming in, I think it's him, yes, it's Vatanen". Two minutes later Rohrl had still not arrived. Ari had taken the lead again, with a minute-and-a-half to spare.

'The atmosphere was magical. No rally had witnessed such a spectacular outcome. But I was thinking of Ari. Never had a driver performed so magnificently. He was truly one of the greats. From that day onwards I was in his debt.'

Peugeot had not won the Monte Carlo Rally for 53 years and all France went wild with delight. Vatanen's victory trail continued in Sweden, where his new team-mate Timo Salonen finished third. It was Vatanen's fifth consecutive win for Peugeot, but after that his victory bubble burst. In Portugal his retirement was brought largely by his own impatience and it was left to Salonen to take advantage of Walter Rohrl's misfortunes and snatch the event from under Audi's nose. Salonen moved into the lead in the World Rally Championship.

In April, the rally circus moved to Africa for the Safari and, for the first time in

The Group B rally supercars raised the 'visibility' of world-class rallying and delighted spectators, especially in Britain. This picture of Kalle Grundel on the Lombard RAC Rally shows why. He and team-mate Timo Salonen retired from the 1985 RAC but Salonen came back to win in 1986.

the competition history of the 205 Turbo 16, Peugeot never led the event at any time, a sad reminder of the team's ill-fated test sessions in Kenya the previous year.

The Safari has never been won by a team or driver in the course of winning a World Championship, and once again it proved the undoing of the supercars, Salonen's Peugeot finally struggling to the finish in seventh place after endless problems, Vatanen retiring with a blown head gasket following a split radiator, and Bruno Saby breaking the third car's chassis. Todt could at least argue that Peugeot had finished the Safari at its first attempt as he looked forward to their next date, the Tour de Corse: 'We were going to celebrate our first birthday there by presenting the new Evolution 2'.

As Martin Sharp has detailed in a previous chapter, the E2 was all about weight loss, improved stability, vastly increased power and specialized aerodynamics; but its appearance in the hands of Saby alone at the Tour de Corse (while Vatanen and Salonen drove the proven E1 version) indicated the misgivings the team still had about the new winged creation. It was the most radical interpretation of Group B rules seen to date.

Corsica was one of those rallies in which Vatanen's behaviour proved hard to fathom. Critically delayed by a double puncture early in the event, he would nevertheless have been assured of regaining third place by the end of the rally; yet instead he allowed himself to be seduced into a 'death-or-glory' run which had a predictable outcome in a lurid accident — whereupon the driver publicly accused his embarrassed co-driver of failing to read the pace notes properly.

In the event, all Vatanen achieved was to prevent Bruno Saby from having the chance of pressurizing the leader, Jean Ragnotti's Renault. But second place still meant 16 valuable points added to the World Championship total, even if it was the second consecutive event on which Peugeot had been defeated.

The Acropolis that followed showed again that Timo Salonen was gaining the ascendancy in the Peugeot team. He won with ease here, while Ari experienced an early steering failure. The team thus departed for New Zealand with Salonen the World Champion elect — a situation scarcely envisaged even by his most ardent supporters at the beginning of 1985.

The 1-2 triumph that followed was the first in the team's short but super-successful history; yet once again it was Salonen in front.

Vatanen's reply in the next event, in Argentina, came on the very first special stage, where he set fastest time. But he never completed the second test, rolling violently end-over-end after hitting a sudden dip in the road and cartwheeling off the track at very high speed. Although the car's basic structure withstood the phenomenal impact well, the driver was so critically injured that he was near to death on more than one occasion after the accident, and was destined not to drive competitively again until the 1987 Paris-Dakar.

In Vatanen's absence, Sweden's Kalle Grundel was co-opted into the Peugeot

While the 205 Turbo 16 was winning rallies overall, the 205GTI achieved considerable success in its Group A class. Britain's fastest lady rally driver, Louise Aitken-Walker, won her class in the 1985 Shell Oils RAC Open Rally Championship, (above), while PTS UK rally star Mikael Sundstrom, (below), impressed racegoers with his third place in the wet at Brands Hatch in a British Saloon Car Championship event on August Bank Holiday 1986.

team for the 1000 Lakes. Despite going off the road on the very first stage, which both angered and saddened his team manager, Grundel salvaged fifth place, while the ever-reliable Salonen took no unnecessary risks while driving consistently quickly to win both the Rally and the World Championship.

Peugeot had beaten the world at their first attempt.

The 1000 Lakes was the first time that the E2 car had been used since Corsica. In the autumn, Peugeot returned to Sanremo, the scene of their major triumph 12 months earlier, and found themselves outclassed by Rohrl and the new E2 Audi Quattro Sport. It was the first time that the French had been beaten in Europe for over a year. Then a superbly successful season ended on a low note, as both Peugeots retired on the RAC Rally.

Vatanen's horrific accident, and similar incidents that befell others in 1985, set alarm bells ringing. Using special fuel additives to boost power and with white-hot turbochargers surrounded by inflammable materials, the Group B machines in their 500bhp second evolution guise were akin to roadgoing Formula 1 cars. They were difficult and tiring to drive and, in conjunction with ever-increasing numbers of spectators, World Championship rallying, said some, was heading remorselessly towards a tragedy. Sadly, there were to be several of them in 1986, including fatal accidents in Portugal and Corsica.

Against this background of impending doom, a relaxed young Finn named Juha Kankkunen joined Peugeot from Toyota and immediately set about the business of accumulating points in the 1986 World Rally Championship.

In Monte Carlo it was Pirelli's turn to win the 'tyre war', to the benefit of Lancia. In Sweden, however, Kankkunen turned the tables, winning the rally on his first-ever visit.

The accidents of Portugal and Corsica were mercifully split by African adventures on the Safari, but here Kankkunen, the previous year's winner, pushed his Peugeot too hard for too long. Two brilliant drives in Greece and New Zealand followed. By September, when Salonen won the 1000 Lakes again and Kankkunen finished second, there was only the Drivers' Championship to fight for; Peugeot had already clinched the Manufacturers' title for the second year running.

With the prospect of Group B cars being banned at the end of the year, Peugeot pushed forward with developments already in hand. The 205 Turbo 16's power output rose towards 600bhp.

It is probable that rally cars were never faster than on the tricky tarmac stages of the 1986 Sanremo Rally; they were certainly an awesome sight to behold. The results of this rally became shrouded in the protests surrounding the Peugeots' bodyside 'skirts'. Ultimately, Peugeot triumphed over officialdom to win both the Manufacturers' and Drivers' world titles for a second year, Timo Salonen's victories on home ground in Finland and in the UK on the RAC being balanced by Juha Kankkunen's three wins in Sweden, Greece and New

With Group B cars banned from the World Rally Championship, Peugeot embarked on a programme of one-off events for 1987. The first was the gruelling Paris-Dakar, attacked with a team of 'long range' 205 Turbo 16s with 12in longer wheelbase (to accommodate a 42-gallon fuel tank), increased track, twin spring/shock absorbers at each wheel and 360bhp engine. Ari Vatanen scored a clear win in what was his comeback drive.

Zealand. The younger Finn was eventually proclaimed Champion.

The Group B supercars were banned from 1987 onwards. The Peugeot 205 Turbo 16 ended its career as a lion on top of the world. It was the most successful car in rallying's fastest and most powerful era.

The achievements of the Group B car have naturally overshadowed the competitiveness of its little brother — the production front-wheel-drive 205GTI. In Group A form, it was always a 'class' competitor rather than outright winner because of its comparatively small engine capacity (which was only extended to 1.9 litres in time for the 1987 season).

With little more than 140bhp available from the 1.6-litre engine, the agile GTI had to be 'pedalled hard' and no-one did that better than Mikael Sundstrom, another young Finn in whom Peugeot's UK team manager Des O'Dell had enormous faith. He put in some spectacular drives with a Group A GTI before the Coventry team took delivery of their first Turbo 16.

In France, the existence of a 205GTI Cup has met with great enthusiasm and advanced the careers of drivers like Couloumies and Delecour, while in Britain the determined lady rally driver Louise Aitken-Walker has achieved good results with a Group A car run from Coventry.

The GTI's Group A specification includes a revised cylinder head and camshaft, special distributor, lightweight pistons, and cylinder liners to allow an overbore to the class capacity limit.

The clutch uses a standard size of pressure plate, but employs different friction material, while the sump is baffled to inhibit oil surge. Peugeot Talbot Sports' spring and damper kit is designed specifically for asphalt use, but PTS UK has employed Bilstein assistance to develop a gravel set-up — the primary difference between the two systems being that the British have opted for Rose jointing.

Brakes are supplied by AP Racing, as they are for the Turbo 16, and comprise four-piston calipers at the front and Peugeot 505 discs at the rear — brakes are 'free' in Group A.

Gears are to French specification and are a close-ratio set, but the gearbox itself still uses the standard roadgoing synchromesh. Peugeot Talbot Sport use an adjustable plate-type limited-slip differential.

In most other respects the little car remains remarkably standard. Driving it competitively for the first time, experienced former rally driver Chris Sclater described the Group A car in *Cars & Car Conversions* thus: 'Everything felt almost perfect on tarmac. The brakes were excellent — a very good pedal with superbly progressive feel. The gear-change was fast and clean with an ideal amount of movement through the gate, while the engine proved to be unfussy and pulled strongly from comparatively low rpm.

'Handling proved very stable and entirely predictable, and it was difficult to get the car to lift wheels under any circumstances, slight understeer being easily remedied by a quick lift of the throttle foot, or by left-foot braking.

'On the loose it felt surprisingly good, even with intermediate-pattern racing tyres fitted. The car has a firm, well-controlled ride, and there's no problem with straight-line stability. The 205 also possesses good reactions to a left-foot braking technique. Brake balance adjustment also worked well.

In conclusion, I would rate this car as a real little stormer!'

Peugeot certainly took the rally world by storm.